PARENTING AND SEX

SUPPORT FOR PARENTS AT ALL STAGES — FROM YOUR

CHILD IS BORN UNTIL BEYOND ADOLESCENCE

by Michael and Terri Quinn

HANDBOOK FOR THE ''PARENTING AND SEX'' PROGRAMME

First published 1991
by Family Caring Trust
44 Rathfriland Road
Newry
Co. Down
BT34 1LD

Copyright c Family Caring Trust, 1991
ISBN 1 872253 02 4

Illustrations and design: Pauline McGrath
Typesetting: Cassidy Printers, Newry
Printing: Universities Press (Belfast)

CONTENTS

BEFORE YOU START

"Sex education? Oh, I'm surprised you haven't dealt with that yet. We crossed that hurdle a long time ago."

Not just facts

In preparing this book, we occasionally came across that reaction from parents. They obviously saw sex education in terms of telling children about "the facts of life." But that is only a very small part of what this book is about. Sex education, after all, is something ongoing, something that begins when a child is born and continues right through adolescence and young adulthood. It includes all parenting skills — listening, talking, problem solving, encouraging, disciplining, and helping children to act with a growing sense of responsibility. It is also one of the very best situations we know of for building trust and getting closer to children.

Unfortunately, some of those who write about sex education have given little thought to the role of parents. They will often shrug their shoulders and say "Yes, it is the parent's responsibility, but parents don't face up to it, so we have to fall back on the school." Even books written specifically for parents tend to present **information** about sex rather than show parents how they might overcome the very real difficulties in communicating about it. The emphasis tends to be on talking rather than on the much more important skill of **listening**. And there is little or no attempt to tie sex education

Sex education,

I'm surprised you haven't dealt with that yet.

into its natural context of bringing up children and parenting in general. A fifteen year old boy who recently experienced a sex education programme at school asked: "Why is there nothing like this for our parents to make it easier for them to talk to us?"

Where does the school come in?

This is not to suggest that the school should not be involved. We assume that children will be learning some very valuable lessons about sex in the school. We take it for granted that the school will be teaching some things which the ordinary parent has neither the information nor the expertise to teach — technical details, biological information, perhaps information about sexually transmitted diseases. But a parent brings an entirely different dimension, and entirely different methods, to sex education. It is no accident that the first chapter is entitled "You don't need much information." Unfortunately, well- meaning authors have sometimes swamped parents with information that actually tended to leave them feeling more frightened, more embarrassed, and more inadequate than ever. A parent's very different (and irreplaceable) task should become clearer as we go through the book.

Emphasis on skills

The emphasis in this book, then, is not on information about sex but on communication skills. This approach has a number of advantages. Some parents look for the "right answers" for their children. But there is no one way to talk about sex or to deal with the various situations parents meet; what suits one parent or child may be quite unsuitable for another. The quiet, shy child, for example, will respond to one approach, while the talkative child may respond to quite a different one. Using these skills allows that flexibility and enables parents to find answers and solutions that respect their own beliefs and suit their own family and situation.

Another advantage of the emphasis on skills rather than on information is that people from different backgrounds and with very different levels of education can feel comfortable — because picking up skills depends more on regular practice than on one's educational background.

Who is this book for?

This book is aimed at all parents, young and not so young, married and unmarried, widowed and separated. Some may feel confident and comfortable with sex education; others may feel they have little to give their child. Some may feel it is too early; others may feel it is too late. Those who are married may feel happily married; others may feel a bit hopeless about their marriages. But we have found that sex education can begin in almost any situation and at any stage — and that these methods work as well for parents of teenagers as for parents of younger children. But don't expect miracles. Reading this book or doing the programme linked with it should be a help, but it is unlikely to make you feel skilled or comfortable immediately. It is only a beginning. It may give you a sense of direction, and a push off in that direction. The skill and confidence will only come with practice.

Throughout the book, there are examples with both young and older children. Parents of young children can benefit greatly from the freedom that comes from thinking and talking about these topics even though they may not meet them for years.

The book may be useful on its own, but it is best used as part of a five session course for small groups of parents. The Leader's Guide for the course is available separately from Family Caring Trust.

You don't need much information.

If this shocks you..

If the book shocks you in parts, it is not because of any desire to shock. It is because the new permissive standards of sexual behaviour are themselves quite shocking to many of today's parents. But young people are very aware of these new standards. There is a real danger of parents burying their heads in the ground, hoping these increased pressures will not affect their children. That would be unfortunate, because our teenage children may disregard us

and see our standards as irrelevant if we are seen to be out of touch, if we are frightened of dealing with the reality of their situation, and just wish it would all go away.

This book is aimed at all parents.

Morality

Much sex education avoids the issue of morality, or does not deal adequately with it. Some sex educators, for example, deal with morality as if it all boiled down to having "safe" sex that avoided pregnancy and sexually transmitted diseases. We have sought, in designing this programme, to respect parents' beliefs and enable them to help their children to form clearer, thought-out values. But it needs to be said that this is done more effectively with questions and with personal statements rather than with "right" answers. The challenge is for parents to deepen their own awareness of their values and of the reasons for what they believe. This deepening will happen to some extent on the course, but parents will do well to read a helpful book or familiarise themselves with the teaching of their own church. For this purpose there are some books recommended in the booklist at the back of this handbook.

No blaming!

There is naturally considerable emphasis on the couple and on education for marriage in a book on sex education. Indeed, there is a special appendix with questions for a couple to talk about. If you are parenting alone, however, there is much in these pages that will help you to feel included and at ease and to see how much you have to give to your children. This is a book for all parents.

We would also like to reassure anyone who may have a sense of failure or who may feel guilty about having neglected sex education in the past. Your children are going to make their own life-choices, including some wrong choices. You must not take the blame for that. All you have done for your children has been well-intentioned — you have cared for them as best you knew at the time. Remember that we are dealing here with an area of life that has been neglected by almost everyone until recently. Why blame yourself (or your own parents) when there was little or no training or support available? The fact that you are reading this now is a sign of your openness and willingness to learn. That is already making a difference. It is so much more helpful to focus on the positive than to beat yourself about the head with guilt.

Acknowledgements

This book, and the programme of which it is a part, would have been impossible but for the co-operation and input we received from a great many people, too numerous to mention individually — from various groups, churches and organisations throughout Britain and Ireland. We would like to express our sincere thanks to all of them. And not least to our own children.

CHAPTER ONE:
YOU DON'T NEED MUCH INFORMATION

"Do you know what else you can do with this? You can stick it up into a woman and get a baby."

That comment was overheard in the toilet block of a small village school recently. The speaker was a seven year old boy and the friend he was speaking to was six. It was an unfortunate introduction to sex, but it is not exceptional.

A great many children of six, seven, eight, and nine now talk to each other about sex. The information is often inaccurate and crude, picked up from television, from tabloid newspapers, from toilet doors, or from other children. You may think your children have been protected from such information, and you may be correct, but many parents who have talked to their children about sex as a result of this course have been very surprised to find out how much their children already knew. That is one of many good reasons for parents to talk to their very young children about sex. It can be a great help to them to have wrong information and wrong attitudes corrected as soon as possible. And it can also make a big difference to hear about sex from you first — research shows that the more open parents are in talking to their children about sex, the less likely the children are to be sexually active as teenagers. Moreover, the younger a child is when a parent talks about sex, the easier it is — and the easier it proves to talk at a deeper level later when the child becomes a teenager.

"I don't know how to talk about sex!"

"That's all very well" you may say, "But sex is a very difficult subject to talk about. I've had no training. I wouldn't know how to cope with some of the questions they might ask!"

One good way to cope is to recognise that you do not need much information. A good question is usually better than a good answer. Indeed, very often the best answer is just to turn a child's question back. Here is an example.

Four year old Virginia Walker was fascinated with the news that her mother was going to have a baby. For days she had kept coming back to her mother, sometimes with little comments: "I think it might be two babies!" and sometimes with questions: "Has she got a little pillow for her head?" or "How will you know when she's ready to come out?" Her mother enjoyed the closeness of these moments.

Then came another question, out of the blue. Mrs Walker froze when Virginia asked her "Where did the baby come from?"

She wanted to tell Virginia the truth, not to give her hang-ups about sex, but how could she tell a four year old child about sexual intercourse?

"What do you think yourself?" she asked, fighting for time.

"I think.. it just grows" was the answer.

"Mm. That's a good guess. It does. It grows from a little egg and seed."

And Virginia went off contented.

Where did the baby come from?

No need to panic.

Mrs Walker's natural instinct was a very good one — to turn back the question. But it is not just a matter of playing for time when you feel you're in a tight corner. No matter what stage your child is at, turning a question back is usually more helpful than giving information.

Many parents are frightened of sex education because they think they need to have a lot of information and be able to explain things clearly and confidently. So they feel inadequate. Whereas the truth is that we need little or no specialised information. This will become more obvious as we progress through this book.

That is also well summed up by one parent who attended this course. "I used to be so frightened of sex education," she said. "I thought it just meant talking about technical things or embarrassing intimate details. Now I just sit down at the table and ask something like: 'I'd like to hear what everyone thinks — when you get married, who'll cook the dinner if you and your partner are both out working all day?' I realise now that there's an awful lot of good sex education in just getting them to think about a question like that. After all, a good sexual relationship means much more than just sharing a bed."

You will notice that Mrs Walker, in the previous example, had also given a very simple (though truthful) answer. Actually, she could have explained things in any one of dozens of different ways, depending on her beliefs and on what she was comfortable with saying: "It grows from a little seed" "Dad put a little seed in there." "God and Mum and Dad made it together." "Dad and I made it — he put a little seed in through my vagina and it joined up with a little egg inside me." More detailed explanations are neither necessary nor helpful at this stage.

Sex education begins when the child is born...

Or when your child is older

Let's look at an example with an older child and see how much better turning back the question can be than giving a direct answer.

Sixteen-year old Diane asked her father "Do you not think sex before marriage is a good idea?"

Her father, as she knows, does not think so. He was tempted to say "No, I don't think it's a good idea!" But he knew that would put a complete stop to further discussion — and that further discussion was the very thing that would help Diane to think more clearly and make good decisions, so he gently put the ball back into her court:

"I'm not sure why you're asking the question?"

She then explained that some of her friends had been putting forward very convincing arguments for pre-marital sex. Her father went on to ask "What do you think, Diane?.." and then "Why do you say that?.."

It was also important for Diane to hear what her father thought, of course, (and we will look at what he might say when we come to chapter three), but he was wise to start by asking questions — otherwise he might never have discovered what she was confused about, and he might not have given her the opportunity to talk that out.

Do you not think sex before marriage is a good idea?

How young should you start?

One of the things that is probably obvious from these examples is that sex education is ongoing — it begins at birth and continues on right through adolescence and young adulthood.

Sex education begins when a child is born. It begins with the sense of being loved and cared for. Children learn so much from the way they are touched, dressed, talked to, played with; they even learn a lot from the toys they are given. They learn how boys and girls are expected to behave, and whether or not it is nice to be a boy or girl, and whether or not they are lovable in themselves — or only lovable when they are "good". (It is good for parents to distinguish between the person and the action — not "You are a naughty girl!" but "That was a naughty thing to do!"). Sadly, they often learn from how we treat them that little boys are expected to be rough and kick balls about, while girls are gentle and play with dolls; that boys are expected to like guns and be "tough", while girls are "soft" and cry easily. "Don't be crying like a little girl!" is the kind of remark that can leave a lasting — and unfortunate — impression on a little boy's mind; in the same way, little girls often feel they have to live up to their "gentle" image even at times when they **need** to be tough. Similarly, lifelong hang-ups about being naked or touching their own sexual parts can result from how we parents behave, how uncomfortable we are with nudity ourselves, and what we say during these early years.

But what should we say? And when? How much information do you give at six, at eight, at ten?..

There are no rules. Every child is different. Every parent is different. Many parents do not even become aware of the possibilities until their children are older. They may feel guilty then, and that is sad — to be guilty about something they were not even aware of and had no training for. Parents don't need to listen to that kind of guilt.

Sometimes its easier to talk when...

In an ideal world..

In an ideal world, however, it would be nice to think that children would just grow up from babyhood with a gradually unfolding picture of how babies are conceived and born, and that they would grow up comfortable with their own bodies and with the knowledge that sex is good and that it is fun. In this way they would be spared the pain and trauma later of trying to digest information about sex that is inaccurate, or too late, or too much, or too sudden, or coming from the wrong sources. By the age of five or six, a child would know about both Dad's and Mum's part in making a baby. Keeping them "innocent" implies that sex is dirty rather than good, and only leaves innocent children at the mercy of others! (It may help to distinguish between innocence, which is the absence of guilt; and ignorance, which is the absence of knowledge). By the age of nine or ten, they would be aware of the full details. It is important, for example, to prepare your daughter for having periods long before her first period arrives. In this way, the frightening "big talk" will not be necessary.

It follows from this that the story of sex is told naturally, bit by bit, building on everyday events like your sister's pregnancy, or the use of slang, or the discovery that your son is playing "Doctors and nurses" with a neighbour's daughter, or questions arising from seeing Mum or Dad nude — rather than in one sit-down session. Honest, simple answers to questions are best ("Why have mummies got breasts?" — "For feeding babies" "How did I come out?" — "Through the special opening between my legs.")

Setting time aside

It may not be a good idea to wait until we are asked a question, however — because the questions may not come directly from some children. A suggestion might be that we choose relaxed quiet times, without distractions, for a chat — like bedtime for a younger child, or over a special supper for a teenager. Lots of things can be talked about during these sessions, including friends, holidays, memories, plans, presents — and sex. For one parent to take one child aside like this can make that child very special — they will often bubble over with questions and stories. Barriers break down. Trust builds up. Parent and child draw closer.

It is harder, of course, for parents of teenagers if they have not talked about sex until now. Go easy on yourself. Lead in gently. A special supper may be too formal. It may just be a question of taking the time to sit down and start a chat instead of rushing lunchtime — "How was the disco last night? What were you wearing?.. What clothes **do** the men wear at discos now?'' Chatting like that can begin to break the ice — and breaking the ice is enough for a start. Sometimes it is easier to talk when you are not facing each other — on a journey in the car, or washing the dishes together. Give yourself time and you'll find what suits you best.

At the end of this book there are some questions which may be helpful for opening up these conversations. The earlier questions in each section tend to be suitable for younger children, the later ones for teenagers. Choose only the ones you feel comfortable with. It often helps to begin a chat by talking from your own experience first (like how you learned, or didn't learn, about sex yourself, even: ''I'm embarrassed, at my age, that I know so little about sex, but that's the way I was brought up''). That can make it safe for a child to open up and trust you. But do take things gradually. Be happy with little steps. It will be chapter three, for example, before we look at how we might talk about sexual intercourse.

How we behave

This book is not just about **talking** to children about sex. It is more about listening than talking. It is more about asking questions than giving information. It is more about how we can help our children to form sound values and make responsible decisions — at all ages — than about giving them mere facts. It is more about good parenting than about sex itself — for that lays the **foundation** for a good sex education! Indeed, how we **behave** may communicate far more than anything we say.

For example, children often get the unfortunate idea that some parts of their bodies are nasty, even though no one has ever said so. Why? Well, two year olds pick up that message when they get a smack for examining their own sexual organs, or perhaps from the look on your face when you are changing a nappy.

But how we behave can also have a very **positive** effect. We have just seen the importance of putting time aside for special chats with children. Making time like this, instead of always sending them off to play, or to watch television — or to eat in front of the TV — can say a great deal to children about how deeply they are loved. They see themselves in a better

light. The entire self-image improves. And that in itself, as we will see, is a very important part of sex-education.

The couple

You will also gain great freedom in chatting about sex with your child when you become freer in chatting about sex to other adults, but especially to your own partner, if you have one. Many people believe that one of the best possible forms of sex education is just exposing a child to an ordinary couple who love each other and are increasingly free with **each other** in talking honestly and personally about their own sex life — including admitting at times that sex is far from perfect for them. So there are also some questions in the appendix at the back for a couple to chat about.

A toddler can feel quite jealous of Mum's and Dad's closeness, of course, and may try to come between the parents, getting into their bed, etc. A couple need to be gentle but firm in resisting this. They should not hide their love for each other. Hugging and kissing each other in front of the children is one very obvious way of showing their love. This actually **helps** children, reassuring them that the marriage is strong as well as letting them see marriage as an attractive way of life. Indeed, if there is a good deal of bickering and fighting in your marriage, it may help to take a child aside occasionally and explain: ''Sometimes I think you see the worst of what goes on between us, but I want you to know that we also have some great moments of closeness.'' That can be quite reassuring to a child.

For the most important lessons your children will ever learn about how men and women should treat each other are probably the lessons you are unconsciously teaching by how **you** treat each other. In the case of single parents, this may be how you treat the other significant people in your life — grandad, a friend, your relatives, etc. In this respect, it may be important for single parents to try to ensure that their children are exposed from early in life to both male and female roles, because research shows that this helps children to form a clearer sense of their own sexual identity and can prevent sexual problems arising later.

TABLE ONE : DEALING WITH QUESTIONS

As trust builds up between you and your child, you may find yourself on the receiving end of many questions. Here are three ways of dealing with some commonly asked questions. Which do you prefer?

CHILD'S QUESTION	PARENT'S REACTION		
	DISCUSSION STOPPER	SHORT ANSWER	TURN BACK QUESTION
WHERE DOES A BABY COME FROM?	YOU'RE TOO YOUNG! I'LL TELL YOU WHEN YOU'RE OLDER (arouses curiosity and makes sex a big "secret").	IT GROWS FROM A SEED. (No need to give big explanation. Better for child to learn little by little).	I WONDER WHY YOU'RE ASKING THAT?... (Reveals what child is hearing, wondering about, or confused about).
DOES THE BABY COME OUT THROUGH YOUR BUM?	DON'T ASK SILLY QUESTIONS (passes parent's discomfort on to child and may give impression sex is dirty).	NO, IT COMES OUT THROUGH AN OPENING AT THE BOTTOM OF MY TUMMY.	WHAT DO YOU THINK YOURSELF? (Not just playing for time — it's encouraging to talk around the subject).
WHAT'S A HOMOSEXUAL?	THE LESS YOU KNOW ABOUT THINGS LIKE THAT THE BETTER! (Betrays parents fears and denies children the opportunity to discuss with parents an issue their friends are talking about).	IT IS SOMEONE WHO IS ATTRACTED TO PEOPLE OF THE SAME SEX.	I'M NOT SURE WHERE YOU CAME ACROSS THAT WORD? (It often helps to explore where a question is coming from).
WHAT'S AN STD?	WHAT WILL YOU ASK NEXT! WHEN I WAS YOUR AGE... (cuts off communication and forces child to look to friends for information — and values).	IT MEANS A SEXUALLY TRANSMITTED DISEASE — A DISEASE YOU CAN PICK UP FROM HAVING SEX WITH SOMEONE WHO HAS AN INFECTION. or I DON'T KNOW. I'LL FIND OUT FOR YOU (Don't be afraid to admit you don't know — you win your child's respect by your honesty).	HAVE YOU ANY IDEA YOURSELF? WHAT DO YOU THINK IT IS? (This is not a substitute for giving information, but can be helpful opening, especially because it encourages 2-way conversation between the young person and the parent).

COMMENTS FROM PARENTS

When I was getting out of the bath, he pointed to the scar and asked me "Is that where I came out?" I said it wasn't. "Where did I come out?" he asked. "You're too young" I said, "I'll tell you when you're older." He never asked again — I think he picked up the vibes that I couldn't cope. He was seven then. He wasn't too young. He was ready, but I was the one who wasn't ready, and it's a barrier between us now. Tell the younger parents that. I wish they could learn from my experience.

When he was four, I told him about God's beautiful plan to make men and women love each other and play and have fun together and be able to share with God in making a baby by their very love for each other. I felt I had to explain it as simple as that, and then I realised myself that it is as simple and beautiful as that. It's we adults who complicate it.

When I asked him what parts he wouldn't like people to touch he said his back bottom, his front bottom and his neck! When I asked about this I discovered he had heard something about children being strangled. I don't think he was so frightened once he had the chance to talk about it.

When I begin to talk about anything to do with sex, he says "We're doing that at school!" or something. He just can't cope with it at all. When he was younger, I didn't want to "spoil his innocence", but I'm sorry now — that was the time to talk.

I still haven't recovered from the shock of my husband getting involved. At first, he was half-scoffing, but very interested to hear how the course was going; then, after the fourth session, he told me he would like to ask Gary some of the questions — and he did. I'm really pleased about that.

It would have been madness to go straight into asking her questions, so telling her a secret helped. I told her how we used to get the boys to chase us when I was thirteen, and how I'd pretend to fall if I fancied a boy so that he could catch me. She loosened up when I told her that.

We were kissing and hugging the children but seldom making time to kiss and to hold each other in front of them. Now that we've changed, I don't know if the children have noticed it yet, but I'm enjoying it!

I told her about periods, making it clear that this was a secret between me and her (because I didn't want her talking to her friends in school before their parents talked to them). When I was finished, she put her arms around me and gave me a big hug.

Without the course I wouldn't have spoken to my eight year old about sexual intercourse (I thought she was too young) and we would both have missed so much. I know she feels closer to me now and I love the way she comes running up to me with a kiss. Sex isn't a dirty word any longer.

It seemed so impossible that I would ever talk to them about sex in a relaxed way. But it was a bit like jumping in for a swim. All kinds of doubts beforehand, then it's normal. I feel much greater freedom with him now.

I told him someone had been talking to me about what boys and girls expected of each other on a date. I said I had never thought about it before, so I didn't know what to say — I wondered had he thought about it? That was a more natural way to start — within minutes he was telling me why he thought so many young women were becoming pregnant. Breaking the ice was everything.

GETTING IN TOUCH

Read the following statement, and have a little chat about the questions that follow.

"I don't remember my parents ever talking to me about sex — though I did get a very strong message that my private parts were dirty and a bit shameful, and that sex was something I wasn't to talk about. So I got my information, some of it accurate, and some of it totally misleading, from boys who were slightly older than me. Later I got my hands on some magazines and books which I read secretly and with shame — but with great interest. I suppose the main messages I picked up were: Sex was something men enjoyed and found very exciting; but nice girls didn't enjoy it. Sex was also something dirty — something to be ashamed of and to be secretive about. And the sad truth is that those messages still have a strong influence on me."

1. Where did I get my information about sex — parents? school? friends? brothers/sisters? books? magazines?
2. What were the advantages and disadvantages of learning like this?
3. What's my feeling now when I think about how I learned?

I don't remember my parents ever talking to me about sex...

CASE STUDY

Your twelve year old daughter, Jane, says to you — "I was thinking about what you told me about making love — When was the last time you and Dad did that?" How would you answer? Tick any of the following responses by parents which you agree with, and then underline the one which most appeals to you.

_____ That's my business!
_____ I'm not sure why you're asking?
_____ Last Monday.
_____ You're wondering how often we make love? How often do you think a couple should make love?.. Why do you say that? Can you think of times when they shouldn't?
_____ That's a private matter.
_____ Another approach?

Have a little chat about what you ticked and why. Respect the point of view of other parents who differ from you. For example, many parents welcome opportunities like this and they encourage their children to talk by asking them further questions — but parents also have a perfect right to say this is a private matter which they choose not to discuss with their children. Others may be glad to get their child to talk more about this question — but they may **also** want to make it clear that this is a private matter for them.

SKILL PRACTICE

Read the situations below and tick each of them — √ if you think it's okay; X if its not okay; ? if you are unsure or can see two sides to it.

_____ 1. 10 year old Amanda is combing her hair in front of the bathroom mirror while her 13 year old brother is having a shower. Father discovers this, is very cross, and orders her out of the bathroom. √ X ?

_____ 2. Three year old Tom comes into the bedroom when Mum and Dad are having sexual intercourse. They take him into the bed with them and hug him before sending him back to his bed. √ X ?

_____ 3. Margaret has decided only to give her children the minimum of information about sex. "The more information people get about sex," she says, "The more they want to try out." √ X ?

_____ 4. The men who work alongside Tina enjoy teasing her about the size of her breasts. √ X ?

_____ 5. Two year old Gary had an erection while his mother was bathing him. She just went on rubbing him all over, penis and all. Was she right. √ X ?

_____ 6. A woman in the train is openly breastfeeding her baby. √ X ?

_____ 7. While playing a game of 'Hospital', a number of children, about four years old, check each other's private parts. √ X ?

_____ 8. Pauline told her five year old daughter about sexual intercourse. Her neighbour is disgusted at what she has done, and says: "That's spoiling her innocence". Pauline replies: "No, sex isn't something dirty to spoil her innocence. Little children should grow up with the facts of life." Was Pauline right. √ X ?

_____ 9. Bill wants to do something about his fourteen year old son's sex education. His wife says it's too late. √ X ?

Now form pairs. Choose one situation to discuss. Ask questions and listen well before you attempt to present your own point of view. Getting the "right" answer is not what is important; listening is what matters — just as listening is crucial when you are talking to your child. When both of you have spoken about a topic, move on to the next one. How would you feel about listening to your teenager on some of these topics? (But be sensitive — ask yourself how your teenagers might feel if you **suddenly** started listening well and giving them good attention!)

PLANS FOR NEXT WEEK

Would you like to mark some of the areas below and plan what changes you would like to make during the next week — the success of the course depends on what you do between sessions. It may help to write down your plans.

1. How will I break the ice, even a little bit, with one of my children this week? — possibly talking about my own "sex education" and the difficulties I experienced myself.

2. Am I creating unnecessary hang-ups in the children by being too private about my own body — undressing, having a bath, etc. Could I even try moving around the house with fewer clothes on? (It's okay to be private about my body, of course — that's my right — but it can be helpful for children to be exposed to both the adult male and female nude bodies, though only in a natural way).

3. On _____ day this week I will have a good chat with one of my children. I could possibly join a younger child at play, or at bedtime.

When might be a suitable time for an older child? (See Appendix One for questions to ask, but only choose some that you feel comfortable with. For parents of younger children, the questions under "Saying no to sexual abuse" may be a good place to start. Parents of teenagers may like to talk to their children about some of the topics just discussed in the "Skill Practice" above, but it may be better not to have a "big talk" — just to chat in general and perhaps lead in to one or two questions).

4. If you have a partner, you may like to choose some questions from Appendix Two.

MY PLANS _____

_____

_____

CHAPTER TWO: FREEING CHILDREN TO LOVE.

Sandra was reading the paper when her six year old son Joe came into the room, white with anger.

"I hate Paul" he said. "I could kill him".

Sandra was tempted to say, as her mother had so often said to her when she was small, "You mustn't hate people".

But she recognised that Joe had very strong feelings. Stifling them wasn't the answer. She would have to let him talk them out before he could listen to any advice.

She put the paper aside, put an arm around him and hugged him in closer to her.

"You're really mad with Paul..." she said.

Tears of rage and hurt came to his eyes.

"I hate him" he said.

"It's that strong"

(Sobbing) "He doesn't care about me... He dumped my skate board in the mud..."

"Your lovely new skate board..."

Bitter tears now flowed down Joe's cheeks and he buried his head in his mother's shoulder. The sobs continued for more than three minutes. When he calmed down, she repeated: "Your lovely skate board.." and the tears started to flow freely again. As the sobs lessened, she said: "That was awful for you!" — and again the intense crying returned. Then he began to calm.

When he looked up, his eyes were actually clear.

"What are you going to do?"

"I'll just have to clean it up."

And off he went out to play again.

I hate Paul. I could kill him.

What our tears are for

What had happened was the most natural thing in the world. Joe had healed himself. Instead of trying to bury his very strong feelings, instead of going around with the pain locked inside him, his mother had allowed him to talk and cry the pain out of his system. That is what our tears are for.

His mother had been very wise to recognise the strength of his feelings, put down her paper, and listen. Not just listen with her ears, but with her eyes and heart. She had actually **encouraged** him to cry; she had helped him to heal himself.

People at any age have great power to heal themselves by crying or talking out their painful feelings. All they need is a caring person to listen and give them good attention. Sadly, many parents do not let their children cry. They distract them ("Look at the butterfly!" "Tell me again what the teacher said about your sums"). They scold them ("No more tears!"). They criticise them ("Don't be a cissy!"). All instead of listening.

Let's look at another example that highlights the importance of listening.

It's more about listening

Mr. Campbell decided it was time to take twelve year old Barry aside and talk to him about sex. He was feeling awkward and embarrassed. He felt he should have spoken to Barry earlier. He realised a face-to-face chat would be very threatening, so he switched off the television and they sat in semi-darkness. As soon as he started talking, however, Barry said indignantly: "I know all about that already!"

Barry had learned a good deal from his friends, but he did not know all about it. The truth is that he could not cope with his own feelings. He felt unsure of himself, embarrassed, also frightened of showing his ignorance. Deep down, he would probably have loved to have been free enough to talk about sex to his mother and father. He wished he didn't feel such panic and so many taboos around the whole subject.

Mr. Campbell sensed his son's feelings.

"Well, let's have a little chat anyway. Who was it that talked to you about sex?..."

What followed was a small breakthrough between father and son. And Mr. Campbell learned by accident an important truth about sex education. That it is more about listening and encouraging a child to talk than about giving information.

Listening, of course, is a skill that is learned with practice. It needs to be worked at. In our books on parenting, we have already looked at ways of improving this skill, so we will not repeat these in detail here. It is probably enough to emphasise just two points: firstly, that it is important to pay attention to feelings; and secondly, that it is very helpful to reflect back in your own words what you hear.

I know all about that already.

Improving your listening

Paying attention to feelings improves the whole quality of listening. It is important to stop what you are doing, to care, really care, and to listen for feelings, for the person behind the words. Listening for feelings makes us more sensitive and understanding. Your daughter or son may be very, very reluctant to talk to you about a first love, for example — precisely because of the mixture of feelings, the romance, confusion, embarrassment, delight, pain, uncertainty, and so on. Yet parents who are unaware of these feelings sometimes laugh or mock at children going through this experience. For something as important as a first love to a teenager (or to a younger child) laughter can be very hurtful, and the child will be less liable to trust in future. But parents who are sensitive to their children's feelings will tend to listen much better — and good listening can be enormously helpful in enabling children to sort out the confusion they feel at a time like that. Listening for feelings can be especially helfpul to boys, in that this helps them to get in touch with their own feelings and move away from the tough, Rambo-like, aggressive image which is often expected of men and which is so destructive of good sexual relationships.

It is not enough to understand. The second stage of listening is to encourage the child to talk, to say more. This is usually done by reflecting back some of what you hear. At times, this may just mean repeating a word or phrase to help the child to continue. It may be enough to say an occasional "Yes" or "Uh huh." At other times, you will want to check out if you are hearing the feeling correctly — in the first example, Sandra had checked out: "You're really mad with Paul.." and that had helped him to open up further. But sometimes silence, or an understanding grunt, is all you need to keep a child talking. Take your time. And judge your listening by its effect.

Aren't feelings dangerous!

Now, this emphasis on feelings is sometimes misunderstood. Most people would probably agree that a central goal of sex education is to help children **not** to act on their feelings, not just to act, for example, on a sexual impulse, but to develop their will power and to become free to choose. Why, then, you may ask, are we putting so much emphasis on listening to children and allowing them to express their feelings?

For something as important as a first love to a teenager...

It is true that we want to encourage children not to bury their feelings — to get them out in the open. But this is not the same as encouraging them to **act** on their feelings. It is exactly the opposite. When you help your son to bring his feelings out in the open, you are helping him to gain control of them. They are no longer a powerful, unconscious force that drives him to act in ways that may be very harmful to himself and to others. A very large body of research shows that people who express their feelings rather than stifle them experience healing from past hurts and gain greater freedom to make choices.

When an unmarried daughter is expecting a baby, for example, and is considering abortion or suicide, it may actually be very difficult for some parents to listen, but it is very important that they show understanding for her pain and encourage her to talk about all options. Otherwise, she is very liable to act on fears she is unable to look at.

Helping children to love

In this respect, the little diagram on this page may be useful to parents talking to their children. It shows two ways of acting. The direct way is an unthinking way to behave. The indirect way allows me to respect myself and others and to make loving choices. Here's an example. Paul called his friend Andrew "Stinkpot". Andrew felt hurt and angry, and he acted on those feelings — he thumped Paul. From then on, Paul got his own back by getting his friends to join him in continuing to call Andrew "Stinkpot", and Andrew had to suffer for a long time for acting on his feelings. But consider what might have happened if Andrew had not acted on his feelings. Instead of thumping Paul, he might have stopped to think. Then he might have treated Paul as a friend by saying something like: "I don't call you names, and I don't like you calling me names. Okay?" This is the diagram:

ACTING ON FEELINGS	ACTING RATIONALLY
I FEEL LIKE DOING SOMETHING	I FEEL LIKE DOING SOMETHING
SO I DO IT	I THINK ABOUT IT
	THEN I CHOOSE WHAT I WILL DO

For we are attempting, in sex education, to help our children to grow in love just as they are growing in their bodies. We want them to see how unbalanced it can be for someone to grow and mature physically but to continue to act on feelings — that acting on feelings is generally a sign of insecurity, stress or immaturity. Sex education has surely failed if children are merely given facts and are not invited to make loving choices and develop more loving, respectful relationships.

How we do this, of course, is not by preaching at our children or merely telling them what to do. We can be far more effective when we choose the right moment and ask questions that help a child to become aware of feelings, to think, and to grow in wisdom. In appendix one you will find many questions that may help. Parents are often surprised and relieved to see that many of these questions are more about how men and women treat each other than about the mechanics of sex. Isn't that the core of sex education!

But she won't talk!

Don't be too discouraged, of course, if you find your child is just not interested in talking. Keep in there, but don't push. Remember how difficult it can be, especially for adolescents, to cope with all the new feelings they have — never mind put them into words. If they don't want to talk about the topics at the end of each chapter, respect their right not to talk and stay open to what **they** prefer to talk about.

The power of listening

It probably goes without saying, in fact, that your questions and your listening do not have to be about sex at all. Taking fifteen minutes to sit down together and look at photographs and listen to the memories they awaken in your child can do enormous good. Or taking five minutes to chat to a child over a cuppa after school. For if sex education is about helping children to grow in wisdom and love, then, as we saw in the last chapter, it comes right back to basic good parenting — with the emphasis on affection, encouragement and effective discipline. And listening.

Listening is very important. It builds trust. Children will trust a parent who listens, who isn't always busy, who doesn't react immediately by advising or scolding: "I told you not to do that! I told you what would happen! Why didn't you do what you were told!" Our listening can build up trust at any time, but trust is easier to build at age eight or nine than at age thirteen or later. Then, when something serious needs to be talked about, the child will come to you because the closeness and the trust will be there already. And even if no crisis arises, the atmosphere of closeness and trust in the home will be providing excellent conditions for children to grow in love.

How we behave

In the last chapter we saw the importance of example. Children will learn to listen and to love much better when they see listening and love in their own homes. If you are impatient and selfish, you will behave the same in bed, no matter how many sex manuals you study — and that does not escape the children's notice. But a couple who are affectionate, who occasionally buy each other an unexpected gift, who make time for chatting and listening to each other, who enjoy touching — and whose sexual contact does not always end in intercourse — are already giving their children a rich sex education. For it has been proven that good sex overflows onto children, and that they pick that up and benefit from the more relaxed atmosphere of your home without ever going through your bedroom door.

This is an ideal, of course. There are also difficulties and frustrations in every marriage. So don't underestimate the good you can do, for example after screaming at each other in the heat of a bitter argument, when you let the children know that you have made up.

Single parents may also feel at a disadvantage in this respect, but they can make up for it to quite an extent by ensuring that their children see them relating warmly to other adults. And it is consoling to note that research shows how children of single parents often turn out more mature than others — apparently because of the extra time the single parent tends to spend with them.

A couple who are affectionate...

TABLE TWO: LISTENING (KEEPING THE DOOR OPEN)

Below are some examples of how parents force their children to close up - or help them to open up. What effect do you think these comments would have on you if you were a child? The listening comments may not be your words, of course - the words will vary with different people and different situations

CHILD'S REMARK	HOW CHILD FEELS	PARENT'S REACTION	
		PUT DOWN REMARK	LISTENING REMARK
Tim: "With his penis? That sounds disgusting."	Uncomfortable and ill at ease with his own body.	"It's your problem if you think sex is disgusting!"	"That sounds off-putting to you.." (Encourage Tim to keep talking).
Seven year old Robert: "I hate girls!"	Feels fearful of what he does not know or understand.	"That's just a stage you pass through." (to adult laughter).	"You don't like mixing with girls." (Allows him to think about what he's saying).
Barbara: "My face is spotty."	Feels inferior, alone, frightened of meeting boys.	"It's just your imagination! No one notices spots." (The parent means well but is not listening).	"That's hard — makes it more difficult to feel good about yourself." (Someone understanding her pain makes her feel less alone).
Sonya: "I've met a nice boy. Malcolm's his name."	Excited, trusting.	"Just you watch him. Boys are only interested in one thing!"	"Great. I'm sure you're excited." (Allows Sonya to express feelings and keeps door open for advice later, if necessary).
Carmela: "I think men and women should live together for a year before they get married".	Puzzled, exploring, testing, anxious to talk about values she hears from her friends.	"That's silly talk. What do you know about it!"	"Mm. That's an interesting point You see advantages in living together.." (Encourages further discussion by developing Carmela's statement, and will lead eventually to looking at disadvantages too).

20

COMMENTS FROM PARENTS

In our house it's very hard to get time on your own with one child so we've decided to have special days for one of the children at a time, ending with a treat and chat in our bedroom. It's about the only way to get them on their own.

I found I had to change and adapt the questions and put my own words on them. They weren't worded right.

Learning to listen to my children and giving them the opportunity to express their opinions made them feel important and needed. The ''us and them'' situation has lessened.

When I asked my daughter what age she thought people should start dating, she said 'seventy' and left the room. It's easy to talk to the other two, but I feel hopeless about getting anywhere with her.

They treated the whole thing as an enormous joke and refused to take the questions seriously. I was hurt and frustrated, but it was my own mistake — I should have talked to them in a natural, casual way, and only to one of them at a time. I don't think I should have told them that I was doing a course.

I don't spend enough time with my children — talking about anything, let alone sex. And the years pass so quickly. By starting when they're young I can influence them step by step instead of trying to give them a crash course in sex when it's too late.

We made several attempts but I think two parents together was too much for him. We got nowhere. I didn't make a breakthrough until I talked to him on his own.

Breaking the ice was everything. I felt awkward and stupid and I'm sure I did everything backwards. But I overcame my fears and broke the ice after all these years. I've finally made the breakthrough.

There were a number of times when I would have left my husband only for the solemn promise I had made before God when we got married. That was what helped me to get over the bad patches — which were mostly the result of P.M.T.

When my daughter went to university, she was suddenly exposed for the first time to arguments about the advantages of living together rather than getting married. She felt she had nothing to say because she hadn't thought about these things before. I had a sense then of having failed her — I hadn't prepared her for this. Sex education is much better before a crisis than in the middle of it.

I hope I didn't show, it but I was shocked to discover what a nine year old had been telling my daughter about sex. The friend was getting all kinds of crude stories from one of these very cheap daily newspapers. I'm sure her parents had no idea of the damage it was doing to leave the paper lying around.

It was just too difficult to start after all these years of silence, so I took your advice and didn't push myself. But I have **listened** a lot better this week. That's a start.

GETTING IN TOUCH

It can often be easy to know how people are feeling just by looking at their faces. With a little practice, then, we can become much more sensitive to how people are feeling — and more understanding. What feelings can you see in the faces below? Check out with the person beside you to see if you both agree.

CASE STUDY

Sixteen year old Lorna comes into the room, white-faced, and tells her parents, in a defiant voice: "Guess what! I'm going to have a little brat of my own!"

What do you think Lorna is thinking and feeling behind the defiant front? Underline any of the following words which you think she may be feeling (or add more words):

Terrible; angry; contented; anxious; brave; embarrassed; trapped; shocked; over the moon; miserable; ashamed; terrified of telling her parents; tender; shattered; vulnerable.

Tick any of the following responses by parents you would agree with, and underline the one which most appeals to you:

_____ A brat! You pup! — you walk in here with news like this and add insult to injury by calling it a brat!

_____ I am shocked. You'll have to give me time to recover. Then we'll talk.

_____ How could you have been so stupid!

_____ (Burst into tears)

_____ Sit down... tell us about it.

_____ Not in this house you're not having it!

_____ (Hug) That's awful for you. You must be going through torture.

_____ Another response?

In small groups of three or four people, have a little talk about what you ticked, why, and what you think a parent should do in a case like this. Respect the point of view of members of the group who disagree with you. For example, some parents may just need time to recover from the shock or to deal with the grief; or some parents may **wish** they could hug their daughter but that may be totally out of the question in their family or situation.

SKILL PRACTICE

Below are some topics for practising listening. Allow the other person to say what they like about any of these topics — thoughts, feelings, stories, personal experiences or whatever.

Do not interrupt or say what you think — just listen and encourage them to say more. Then, after a minute or so, sum up in your own words what you have heard, checking out that you have understood them correctly. Do not discuss the topic at this stage, because this is a **listening** exercise. Then choose a new topic and reverse roles.

Men have a lot to lose from women's liberation.

At 70 years old you won't, and shouldn't, be interested in sex.

Men and women should play equal parts in rearing children.

Boys get less sex education at home because they need less.

There should be ongoing sex education in all schools.

The way children treat their families is the way they'll treat their husbands/ wives in the future.

PLANS FOR NEXT WEEK

Would you like to mark some of the areas below and plan what changes you would like to make during the next week — the success of the course depends on what you do between sessions. It may help to write down your plans.

1. Take out some family photos and spend a while talking and answering questions about them — especially photos of you before, during, and after the child was born. (Don't worry if the subject of sex doesn't arise — the point is that you are building a closer bond with your child and developing more trust. And it may be a good opportunity to practise listening. If a child is not open to talking to you, what about planning an outing together to a cinema, cafe, sports centre..?

2. Chapter two makes it clear that the level of affection and touch in the home is an important part of sex education — for sex education has a lot to do with preparing children for warm, loving, human relationships with both sexes. It may help to ask yourself this week, then, how you could show more affection and warmth to both adults and children in your home.

3. You might look, too, at how welcome you make your children's friends — at all ages and stages. Teenagers especially can have healthier,

more open relationships when their friends of both sexes are made welcome in your home.

4. On ____ day this week I will have a good chat with one of my children. Bedtime may be suitable for younger children. What might be a good time for an older child? (It may not be helpful to have a "big chat" about sex — it's probably better to chat in general first about friends, etc., but see Appendix One for questions to ask, and choose one or two that you would feel comfortable with. If your children are not open to talking to you, you can't force them — but many of these questions can be asked casually — at the start of a meal, for example, you could start a discussion on what makes a good husband).

5. If you have a partner, you may like to choose some questions from Appendix Two.

MY PLANS _____

_____

_____

CHAPTER THREE: TALKING ABOUT SEX.

Colin and Elizabeth Farrell had not found it difficult to tell their daughter Sarah about how Sarah had grown inside her mother's womb, about labour, and about her birth. But it was difficult for them to bring themselves to talk about sexual intercourse.

When Sarah was nine, her mother sat on her bed one evening at bedtime and brought up the subject.

"You remember, Sarah, we told you how your Dad and I both helped to make you — that it was Dad's seed that grew inside me. Did I ever tell you how that happens?

"I don't think so."

"Well. We love each other — and we show our love in lots of different ways. Can **you** tell me some of the ways...?

"You hug."

"Yes... Anything else?"

"You talk."

"Yes?.."

"You kiss"

"Yes. Do you like to see us kissing and cuddling?"

"Mm. But not when someone else is here — like Aunt Carol."

"I'll have to remember that. But we do like to kiss and cuddle and hold each other close. The best place is in bed, where we can be closer.

Before we got married, that's one of the things we were most looking forward to — being so close, with nothing between us. Can you understand why that means so much to us?

"Mm."

"Well, sometimes, we hold each other close in a special way so that Dad's penis comes into my vagina and his seed flows in to meet a tiny little egg that's inside me. When the seed meets the egg, a new life begins. That's how you began. We call it making love."

There was a look of shock on Sarah's face.

"I don't believe you" she said "I mean... Yuk. It's disgusting."

"I thought it was strange too when I first heard it", her mother said.

"But it is kind of disgusting" Sarah said.

"You told me some of the girls in your class think breastfeeding is disgusting", her mother reminded her. "But **you** know it's a lovely closeness between a baby and it's mother. Well, its a bit like that with making love. I just love cuddling and being cuddled in bed with Dad — for us there's a lovely closeness and specialness about making love."

"Mm. I didn't think of it that way...."

Half an hour later, Sarah was speaking to her older sister.

"Mum and Dad told me how babies are made. At first I thought it was yuk, but now I can see how it can be lovely and close.."

Sex has their blessing

It would have been more helpful if Sarah's parents had started earlier (younger children take this information much more in their stride) and introduced her to sexual intercourse more gradually — it is better, if possible, not to give too much information in one session. For a parent who is alert, there are many opportunities to have a little chat about sex; the use of slang words, a scene on TV, even innocent sexual experimentation with boys and girls of their own age — but sometimes parents have no choice but to introduce the subject because some children never ask these questions directly.

Nevertheless, Sarah was lucky. Many young boys and girls of her age have already heard about sexual intercourse from friends at school. The explanation is often crude and incomplete. If the young person feels disgusted, there is no one there to talk them through that first reaction, so they can remain stuck, sometimes for life, with a "sex is dirty" attitude.

Did I ever tell you how that happens?

Sarah was also lucky in that her parents' very act of talking about sex was itself a message to Sarah that they saw sex as something good, something that had their blessing — whereas **not** talking about sex might have given the opposite message.

Not to give too much information in one session...

The words we use

The words used by Sarah's mother may not be your words, of course. If your child does not know what 'penis' or 'vagina' mean, you may prefer to talk about Dad's 'willie', 'the opening at the bottom of Mummy's tummy', or whatever words are normal for you. Parents have to be comfortable and find their own way of saying things. However, it is recommended that children get used to hearing the proper words from the start — using 'baby' words often betrays our discomfort, and children are not slow in picking that up. There are diagrams and words in Appendix Three at the back of this book — use these for yourself or along with your child if that helps. In larger bookshops there are also many simply-written, helpful books on the facts of sex that you may like to read or share with your child.

It is also recommended that you explain the meaning of the slang words your child is hearing. It is very helpful to talk about these words — your children may be surprised to hear you "mention the unmentionable", but that can actually help to break down some of the secrecy and mystery surrounding such words and can spark off some great conversations. Chatting about these words can also help children to

distinguish between caring and hurtful attitudes to sex, especially when you speak personally (see Appendix One for questions about slang).

Say how you feel

Did you notice how Sarah's mother spoke on a personal level? That can make a big difference. Don't be afraid to admit, as Elizabeth Farrell did, that you actually make love yourself. Don't be afraid to say how you feel ("I love being cuddled"). Facts are not enough. You can say that a man has a penis and a woman has a vagina, but it can be a lot more difficult to say "I have a penis" or "I have a vagina", because that makes your statement personal. And yet we have to overcome the taboo against speaking personally if we are to be effective in the sex education of our children.

In his book, "Families and how to survive them", Professor Robin Skynner says that parents who do talk to their children about sex tend to give no more than facts, to leave out their feelings. He goes on to say that these parents are leaving out the **crucial** thing, for it is the feelings that really matter. Mere facts about sex and birth control give a very limited "sex education" and offer little in terms of responsibility, meaning and happiness in a sexual relationship. When parents talk on a personal level, when they share their experience, their beliefs, and the reasons why they behave as they do, they can have an enormous influence on their children and can help them to be more at ease with sex and to form clearer, more responsible values and convictions.

Talking to teenagers

We'll look now at an example of how parents talked on a personal level to an older child.

Jim is seventeen and his father makes a point of having little chats with him from time to time. Over the years these chats have often been about sex. One day, Jim told his father about something that had been bothering him for some time — the very strong pressure he was under from his friends to have sex.

"Almost all the boys have sex. They make fun of me and say I must be gay. I can't stand it."

It was obvious that he had very strong feelings, so his father said little; he listened, and helped Jim to say more.

"That's very tough for you..."

"Yeah. If you go out with a girl three times and you don't tell the guys all about how you laid her, they think there's something wrong with you. I really hate it when they make me feel so small."

His father encouraged him to talk on. He did not reassure Jim ("There's nothing wrong with you") or offer advice ("Just tell them you like your girl well enough to go out with her three times and **not** have sex with her'') There would be time for that later — Jim had to talk out his frustration and confusion and sense of isolation first.

When he was finished, his father said:

"Jim, I'm really glad you treat girls with respect — that you don't have casual sex with them. For your Mum and me the very act of sexual intercourse says ''I'll love you as long as I live''. That's what it means for us. So I would never want to give myself totally like that to any other woman. I wouldn't be showing respect either to her or to myself.''

Instead of arguments

Like Sarah in the first example, Jim was lucky. Lucky because he had met someone he trusted, who could listen to him first, but who also had strong values and was able to speak to him about them on a personal level. Jim's father might have given his son lots of good arguments for not having casual sex, but it is unlikely that any of them would have been as powerful or as helpful as his own personal statement.

Can you remember a time when you were chatting to someone who presented a point of view different to your own? Did it stop you in your tracks and make you think — ''Maybe there's more to this than I had realised. Maybe I haven't all the truth?'' That is the effect you can have on your children when you state how you honestly think and feel about things. People can argue for hours about the pros and cons of any subject, but when they meet someone who talks to them honestly on the level of feelings, that tends to make a much greater impact on them and often helps them change their outlook. Your teenage son, for example, may talk at length on the merits of living together as opposed to being married, but when you say: ''I love being married to your father'', the discussion can move onto an entirely different plane.

Not your hang-ups

Now, talking personally should not give parents an excuse for passing their own hang-ups onto their children (like ''All this nudity around the house disgusts me!'') In the first example in this chapter, Sarah had picked up — from somewhere, perhaps from her friends — that there was something disgusting or shameful about the sexual organs. People who think like that can very easily give negative messages to their children. It is better to teach modesty in terms of covering the body, not out of shame, but out of respect for it as something good. Similarly, teaching children to be on their guard against sexual abuse should be set in a positive context of ''good touches'', etc. (see ''Saying No'' in Appendix One). An unexplained ''Don't let anyone touch you there'' may only frighten children or make them think that their private parts are shameful.

This applies equally to older children. If you do not want your son to read girlie magazines, it is not enough to forbid them without giving a positive reason like: ''I hate those magazines because they don't present sex as the act of love it should be — and it seems so unfair to me the way they treat women as nothing more than sex objects.''

Some parents may feel inadequate.

If you feel inadequate

Some parents may feel puzzled when they hear of personal statements about sex. "Where do these parents live who talk to their children like this?" they may ask. The truth is that the vast majority of parents have great difficulty in talking to their children about sex, even in giving basic information or talking about facts — never mind talking personally. But it may be important to remember that we are living at a time of great discovery and change. Many things that were unthinkable in the past are today becoming realities. It is the same with family relationships and communication. We are only now becoming aware of the immense possibilities for encouraging children's growth and development within families. It is an exciting prospect that is already becoming a reality in the homes of people who have attended parenting, marriage, or personal growth courses and worked at the new communication skills. This should be a cause for hope, and not for anxiety, guilt or inadequacy.

Some parents **may** feel inadequate, of course — they may be convinced of the value of talking personally, but they may feel at a loss, and wonder **what** to say. We suggest that you trust your own instinct and start practising, even admitting: "I'm sorry I get all flustered when I talk about sex to you — it's just that my parents never talked to me about it." That in itself can be quite a powerful personal statement. You will find further examples in Table Three.

I get all flustered when I talk to you about sex...

Cropping up naturally

It is also important to recognise that you are probably **already** speaking personally to your children. You see, personal statements will not always come neat and parcelled as in Table Three. They crop up naturally in many of the little chats parents have with their children. For example, talking about how your sister and her husband separated, you might say: "I've heard my sister's story, and I know there are always two sides to a story, so I don't want to give you a one-sided account. I know they're both really good people. John is very sincere, and you know how thoughtful Ann is. What I think happened is this..."

Can you see how many values come across here because you are speaking at a personal level? Appreciation for both people. Unwillingness to gossip. Fair-mindedness. Understanding... And at the same time a story like this can be so much better than a lecture in giving your daughter or son a realistic picture of marriage and family relationships and how these can be dealt with.

Good sex education, then, is not so much about facts as how to handle the facts. Our goal is to help our children form responsible values. Telling the facts, as we have seen, is a great start, and is itself a very positive message coming from parents. But something important is being left out when we merely give facts without feelings and values. Indeed, it is increasingly being recognised that one of the reasons why children are often emotionally immature today is that they are being left so much with other children, and are not being exposed enough to adults and their values.

They'll test out the information!

Some people object that children get too much information about sex today and that this only encourages them to test it out. But such testing happens because of the **influences** on a child — not because of information. Consider, for example, all the influences we pick up from the unquestioned, act-on-your-feelings attitudes to sex on television — which probably do much more damage than all the close-ups of sexual intercourse! Besides, in today's society children are going to get the information anyway. Isn't it much better that parents should also present **their** points of view and use **their** influence?

But where do you draw the line? Should you expose your children to information about things you consider immoral — perhaps abortion as a way of dealing with an unwanted pregnancy? But if you do not tell them about the choices that are available to them — including your feelings about these choices — then they will talk to others instead, and you may lose the opportunity to influence them.

Other support

It is not easy today to help children form responsible attitudes and values. We are swimming against the current, against the enormous influence of the media and of the teenage culture and peer group. That is why it is can be so important to have some kind of support group like the one envisaged by this programme. Parents can then feel strengthened by the sharing and support of others. Some of the books recommended in the back of this book may also be useful in helping us to think about and clarify what we do believe and why.

There are also some books recommended there which can be given to teenagers and which have helped to encourage and support young people in withstanding pressure and forming responsible sexual values.

Another thing that has proved helpful has been to encourage your teenagers to join a local youth group where there are opportunities to think and talk about sex and relationships in a positive context — in a church group or club, Young Men's/Women's Christian Association, etc. Happily, such opportunities are increasingly common.

Your own attitude to sex

Finally, as in previous chapters, it may be important to look at your own attitudes and behaviour. If sex gives you fun and joy, don't hide the fact — let it bubble over and be obvious to your children.

On the other hand, it will be difficult to talk convincingly about the joy of sex if you have lost interest in sex yourself, or if you are going through a difficult patch in your marriage. If you have lost interest in sex, it may be because you are working too hard, unable to switch off work at home, or not getting enough sleep. Or it may be that you need to forget about all the myths about sex — that a man should always be ready, that mutual orgasm is essential, that sex should be spontaneous, not planned for — or that sex should be at night. These myths are harmful when they create unreal expectations that can be difficult to live up to. No one can tell you what sex should be like for you — not how, nor when, nor how often. It is always better to talk out your expectations together and set your own standards.

If you are separated or divorced, or if your marriage is unhappy, you may think you have little to give your children in terms of education for marriage. But we have just seen how a painful situation like a marriage breakdown can be used very positively to help children form values. You do not have to be perfect. Your willingness to speak personally and be very real with your children, your lack of bitterness, your forgiveness, your understanding, are all part of what you have to give.

If you are a single parent, your children may be pleased to have you all to themselves, but it is important for you to talk personally too and to keep your children in touch with your own loneliness, not by constantly harping on it, but by sharing your feelings from time to time. Otherwise, you may feel trapped between "loyalty" to your children and the need for an adult relationship.

For widowed parents, being open and real may also mean not making your late partner sound like an angel — or it may be too discouraging for your children to try to live up to that ideal!

TABLE THREE: TALKING ABOUT SEX

*In the table below there are examples of the difference between giving information and talking personally. There is a place for both — there will be times when basic information may be just what your child needs, but parents also make a unique and special contribution to sex education when they talk on a personal level. Obviously, different people will speak personally in different ways, and the statements below may not reflect your values or your ways of talking. But what effect do you think each of these statements might have on your daughter or son? What **values** are the parents communicating with their personal statements?*

GIVING FACTS/INFORMATION	TALKING PERSONALLY
"Screwing" is a slang word for sexual intercourse.	I'd prefer you not to use that word "screw". It offends me as a woman. (and explain)
About once a month, an egg is released. If it meets the man's seed, it becomes a tiny baby — called a foetus — and sinks into the lining that has built up in the womb to receive it. If the egg and seed don't meet, the egg comes away along with the lining in the womb. That's why a woman has a monthly period.	Every month a little egg is released into my womb. One month we made love just at the right time, so your Dad's seed meet the little egg — and that's when you began. We weren't sure until my period didn't come and I visited the doctor. You can't imagine how excited we were! I loved you being so close inside me for most of a year.
The I.U.D. is a loop or ring you leave in the womb to prevent a baby being conceived — or in some cases it may abort the fertilised egg.	I like natural things — I just don't like using artificial methods, especially anything that might cause abortion. That saddens me.
People are often the victims of their own upbringing. Many men in our society have been brought up to ignore feelings and prove how "tough" they are by drinking and treating women as sex objects.	You know we're not happily married. I wish I was — for your sake as well as my own. And it's not that your father is a bad person — his upbringing was very tough, and very different to mine. Remembering that helps me to forgive him.
Natural family planning is not as safe as the pill, especially when people take risks and don't follow the method — which tends to happen a good deal. The method depends on observing your own body signs — mucus, temperature, etc.*	I'm nervous of natural methods, because there's a greater risk of having a pregnancy that I don't want. What I like about them is that they help me to know my own body and what's happening to it.
One partner may be slower about coming, so the other needs to slow down and be tender and take time. In that way they can come at the same time, which is a much richer experience.	You know I love your Dad and that I'm completely committed to him. That's what sex is all about for me — even when we're not very sexy or don't have mutual orgasm.
There are so many children being born into the world today that the population keeps doubling — and that's causing enormous problems.	I have my off-days, when I wish I'd never had children. But I love you, as you know, and sometimes I have a real pain at the thought that I'll never have another child like you, I have really been very privileged.
Before menstruation, some women can feel terribly depressed or tense, and they almost become like different people.	I'm sorry for screaming at you. At this time of the month I can hardly cope with myself because of the way premenstrual tension affects me.
When a couple get into heavy petting, the lure of sex becomes very attractive and powerful, and it becomes very difficult for them to stop. The result is often casual sex between two people who are not committed to each other. Then they often feel guilty — and cheated by their own sex drive. Whereas committed lovers usually feel at peace after lovemaking.	For me, sexual intercourse is a special act of love between two committed people, and it tears me apart to see couples giving themselves so easily to each other without that commitment. I would hate to see you not respecting yourself like that — but I wouldn't hold it against you, I wouldn't stop loving you if you did get carried away!

* See Appendix Three

COMMENTS FROM PARENTS

I remember saying to my daughter "If you're going to have sex, just be sure you take precautions." But the truth is that I don't want my daughter having casual sex and what I was saying wasn't helping her to understand my values or how I felt.

I told my nine year old I didn't like him watching those films because James Bond treated women as if they had no brains. "But Mummy," he said, "The women in those films don't have any brains!" He was right, you know.

I told him I had my first baby before I married his father. I didn't justify it. At least it wasn't casual sex, I said, but I was sorry it had happened like that, and I wouldn't like him to make the same mistake.

We told John about sexual intercourse at the time, but two years later we discovered by accident that he hadn't understood. It just shows the need for sex-education to be ongoing.

I asked him directly "Have you had sex with her?" He said he had, but that he took precautions. "That's not the point," I said, "You know we believe that sex is a commitment for life." He answered me that I was old-fashioned." "I love you." I said, "And I hate to see you hurting yourself — and her." I knew in my heart he wasn't going to change, but I felt it was important to say what I believed. I hope he will change in the long run.

It was hard for me to say, but I told him that we had made love the previous night and that it had brought us much closer. Isn't it funny that we have no qualms about letting the children see us fight, but we can be so afraid to admit that we also make love.

Talking about slang words was what led to the breakthrough with my thirteen year old. I would say it has transformed our relationship. And we can also tease each other now.

I had been nervous of re-marrying, in case my son couldn't accept a step-father, but when I told him how special his dead father had been to me he said, "Mum, you should get another special friend like that."

I'm glad children are getting more information today — I thought the placenta was a beach in Spain till I was pregnant with my first baby.

When I asked him if he thought a seventy year old should be interested in sex he said certainly not, that it was disgusting. I didn't argue with him but said I hoped his dad and me would still love each other as much when we were seventy and that we'd still enjoy making love. I hope that made him think. It's new for me to talk personally. It was a good question because it helped me to see that he saw sex as something dirty.

I had always seen our sexual relationship as something private, so I was uncomfortable with the idea of talking **personally** about sex. Now that I've started, I can see it's important to actually admit that we make love quite often and what it means to us. I mean, I even discovered that my thirteen year old son thought we had only made love three times — because we had three children!

It was a great idea to start by talking about the sexual slang words — Joseph couldn't believe what he was hearing. He was so amused. He just relaxed right away and told us a few new slang words we hadn't heard and then we had a good talk.

She wouldn't sleep with her boyfriend, and he broke off with her. She was very upset. So I gave her "I married you" by Walter Trobisch. She read it on the train that night, and when she came home she said: "Thanks a lot for that book. It helped me to see that he wasn't right for me."

GETTING IN TOUCH

The following slang words are in common use, and your children are probably hearing or using some of them regularly, so it is very useful for a parent to be aware of them and open to talking about them. Many parents have found a chat about slang a good way to begin talking about sex as well as an excellent way of building trust and helping a child understand the attitudes behind these words:

A. **Sexual intercourse** — fuck, screw, shag, knock up, poke, jump, shaft, bang, score, stuff.
B. **Homosexual** — puff, homo, fag, fairy, bum-chum, fruit.
C. **Male organs** — dick, cock, knob, meat, balls, willie.

D. **Female organs** — cunt, fanny, flap, diddies, pussy.
E. **Masturbation** — jerk off, toss, jack off, frig, toss off.

1. See if you can arrange the following words, one under each of the above headings: tits; queer; ride; wank; prick.
2. What other words can you add under each heading?
3. Look at the slang words for sexual intercourse. Can you see how some of them bring out the idea that males are dominant, active, even cruel, while women are inferior and passive — mere sex objects to be used? How do you feel about that?

CASE STUDY

Mrs Walshe is watching TV with her teenage son and daughter when a very sexy scene comes on, involving a man and woman who are completely nude. What should she do? Tick any of the following approaches you agree with and underline the one which most appeals to you.

____ "Uhh!" an uncomfortable grunt to show you disapprove.
____ "It makes me sad to see people giving themselves to each other like that without being committed to each other."
____ "Turn off the television. That's disgusting!"
____ "This offends me — such an intimate thing presented in such detail in public."
____ Keep an embarrassed silence and hope it will be over soon.
____ "I wonder what's on the other channel?"
____ Remain silent at the time, but make one of the comments above afterwards.
____ "It upsets me how television can catch people's attention with the quick thrill when there's so much more at stake."
____ Make no comment and leave it to the children to make their own judgements
____ Another approach?...

In small groups of three or four people have a little chat about what you ticked and why. Respect the points of view of those who differ from you. Some will turn off the television; others will prefer to make a comment. There is no one right way to handle this situation — people's personalities and backgrounds and circumstances are so different. But what advantages do you see in talking personally (i.e. not leaving out your beliefs and feelings) — at least after the film?

SKILL PRACTICE

1. You have already talked to your thirteen year old son Robert about sexual intercourse, but you are conscious that he is hearing a lot of sexual slang, so you would like to have a chat about these words, what they mean, and how you feel about them. Some of the questions below may help:

I'd like to have a little chat about the ''rude'' words you hear. How I learned them myself. What ''rude'' words have you heard people using?.. (Explain them, or promise to find out). What's wrong with these words? (Bring out how words like screw, lay, bang etc. humiliate women, make them objects instead of persons, and emphasise male dominance). How I feel about them. Do you know the proper names of boys'/ girls' private/ sexual parts? (It may help to use the diagram in Appendix Three for explaining).

Additional skill practice. Think of some of the situations you meet — or are liable to meet — and try making up suitable personal statements that communicate your values in these circumstances.

PLANS FOR NEXT WEEK

Would you like to mark some of the areas below and plan what changes you might like to make during the next week — the success of the course depends on what you do between sessions. It may help to write down your plans.

1. Any new skill will feel a bit strange and awkward at the beginning, but it quickly becomes second nature. You could practise making up personal statements this week — even if you don't get around to using them — but aim at making at least one personal statement to one of your children each day. They can make a big difference.

2. Another area that it may help to look at is television. There's a lot of ''sex education'' by television going on in your home for better or for worse. Do the children watch TV alone in adult viewing time? How do you think you should react to sexual scenes on the screen? (Switch off the TV? Watch in silence? Make a comment? Talk about it afterwards?)

3. On ____ day this week I will have a good chat with one of my children. Bedtime may be

suitable for younger children. When might be a suitable time for an older child? (See Appendix One for questions to ask — ''sexual slang'' may be a good topic because it builds trust in a younger child when these ''unmentionable'' words they are hearing are explained by parents. Talking about slang is also a great opener for a discussion on sex with teenagers — one parents jumbled the words in the ''Getting in Touch'' section above and asked his teenager to try arranging them under the correct headings!).

4. If you have a partner, you may like to choose some questions from Appendix Two.

MY PLANS _____

_____

_____

CHAPTER FOUR: DEALING WITH PROBLEMS

"George, I want to talk to you about Clive. I'm not very happy about your friendship with him."

"How do you mean?"

"Well, maybe it's because he's a few years older than you, I don't know, but I don't like what happens to you when he's around. I feel uneasy about all the giggling and whispering and strange behaviour. And I'm puzzled by it — it's not like you; you're usually so open with us."

Facing up to tensions

Mr Simmons was speaking to his eight year old son, George. Since last spring, when they had completed a parenting course, Mr and Mrs Simmons had begun to have regular sit-down sessions (a half-hour "family meeting") with their son. These were opportunities to talk out decisions affecting George and give him a say in them. Everybody was free to bring up any plans or decisions they wanted to talk about. George

enjoyed these meetings. They gave him a chance to talk without interruption and to experience being listened to, and he had been able to claim greater freedom in exchange for taking on some responsibilities. But now, as happened occasionally, **he** had to listen to one of his parents challenging his behaviour. He would have a chance to present his own point of view, of course, and to talk out a solution to the problem.

What Mr Simmons was doing was very important. Instead of making the mistake (which parents are often tempted to make) of buying peace rather than face up to tensions, he was bringing the tension out into the open for a reasonable, fair discussion. Instead of sniping at his son or getting at him with critical put-downs, he had waited for a time when the tension could be talked about in a calmer atmosphere. He was now open to listening and working to find a solution to the problem, and he had begun, not with a lecture, but by speaking personally — at the level of feelings. It is in this kind of respectful atmosphere that parent-child sex education happens best.

A bumpy journey

Tensions will not always be talked out in a formal, relaxed setting, of course. Because we are human, there will be times when tensions will be shouted out in angry standing-up rows. Don't be too hard on yourself if you lose your head occasionally — most of us do. But even an angry shouting match is usually better than avoiding the tensions and pretending they are not there.

You may also have to be prepared to deal with children who refuse to talk to you or who are too upset for words. When your daughter is in the throes of her first love, the most important thing you may be able to do for her is just to respect her and take her seriously. It may be helpful for her to hear your own experience, and she may gradually feel free to open out and trust you — or she may not. Like most parents, you may feel hopeless at times, and see yourself as a failure; parenting, especially of adolescents, is a bumpy journey for most of us.

Skills for dealing with family tensions are well worth practising, however, for they have been enormously helpful to many parents. Let's look in more detail now at how we can use them. It may help to begin by looking at how one parent dealt with the tension between herself and an older child.

I refuse to talk to you...

Late night party

Joan is fifteen and lives with her single mother. She has to be home for ten thirty each evening, but her mother does make exceptions for special occasions.

Joan's friends have asked her to a party, and she would love to go, but it won't be over until two or three in the morning.

In a case like this, many parents will say: "No. It's out of the question!"; others will say "Okay, no problem." In neither case do the parents have to think very much.

Joan's mother is not like that. Like many thinking parents, she honestly is not sure what to do. So she listens to Joan and finds out more. Who is organising the party? Where will it be? Are there any adults around? Will there be drink at the party? Who will be there? How old are they? Who will drive you home? What will you do if the party gets out of hand?

At the end of all the listening, Joan's mother still is not sure what to do. She tells Joan she can't help worrying — there will be drink at the party, and the people going are mostly older teenagers. But then she has to admit — and she does admit it — that Joan has shown herself pretty responsible recently. She tells Joan she would like to trust her, but she is also conscious that Joan has not had to stand up to very strong pressures before. She just does not know what to do, she says.

Could they work out a compromise? she wonders. Is there anyone else who could drive her home? Would it be possible to leave the party at twelve thirty? Are there other options?.. They take a while to think together about possibilities...

At the end of it all, Joan's mother comes to a decision. What she decides is not what matters, because, whatever it is, the decision will be thought out and responsible. Joan will be involved in it — though she may not be completely happy with it at the time — and she will be more aware of what is at stake. Joan will also be stronger, more thoughtful herself, clearer about the underlying values. And above all, she will know that her mother cares about her, loves her, and wants the best for her.

A more difficult way

Notice what has happened here. Unlike the first example, Joan needed to talk first because the problem was hers. So her mother, instead of making a snap decision, wisely began by asking questions and listening. Only then did she say what she thought and felt herself. In that way, both sides got a chance to have their say and be listened to. Then they explored possibilities together — before they finally came to a decision. This is a method recommended by many parent organisations and parent educators. It is a more difficult, but much more rewarding, way to be a parent. You can see the stages outlined more clearly in Table Four.

Don't be afraid to draw the line

There is something else to notice in this example. Limits were set. Sometimes books on parenting — and on sex-education — give the impression that everything boils down to communication. Communication is very important, of course — listening, talking, exploring, discussing, and encouraging. But parents also have to **act**. Limits need to be set. It is preferable, as in the case above, that the limits be talked out first and the young person involved in the decision-making. But sometimes parents will have to step in themselves and decide what the limits are. For a great deal of research shows that limits are as important for teenagers as they are for young children — even when these limits are only giving the teenagers an opportunity to rebel and kick out and in that way discover who they are. So don't be afraid to draw the line firmly and clearly. In that way you give your children security. They may resent rules, but they will resent the absence of rules even more.

We do adolescents no favour, then, when we give in to their whims and allow them to grow up too fast, when we give them adult rights without adult responsibilities. As long as they live under a parent's roof, they need to be faced into their responsibility for coming-in times, household chores, leaving the bathroom tidy, etc. In this respect part of sex education may be to train boys to cook and wash, and to train girls to use a screwdriver and change a wheel.

You may feel hopeless at times and see yourself as a failure...

Limits and sex education

Children need the security of limits, even when, in their teens, they kick against these limits and challenge many of your beliefs and values. They may not be **aware** of what is happening, but they will frequently test you to find out where you draw the line. It may be something like three year old Judy putting her hand down the front of her panties after being told not to do that in public. She may want to know if you really mean it. Remove her hand, explaining that people do not do that in public, but don't give her a negative message by saying something like "Shame!" or "Dirty!" In that way, your firmness and patience teaches her good manners without giving her hang-ups about sex (just as you might teach her not to pick her nose in the street). It is the same with bad language — it can be corrected like any other form of bad manners. But beware of giving a double message by laughing at your child saying a four letter word — indeed, some behaviours are best **ignored**, particularly when you suspect that correcting them is giving children the attention on demand they may be looking for. Remember the last time you were ignored by

someone? — you probably smarted for the rest of the day. Ignoring a behaviour is not the same as approving of it!

In other ways, too, limits can be a vital part of sex education. Children and adolescents may need to be protected from themselves, from the enormous pressures of the media and of their immature friends. It is not good to have too **many** rules of course, but there does have to be some control on parties, dating, coming-in times, videos, harmful friendships. It is not a question of merely holding back evil. The emphasis needs to be on developing a sense of responsibility and helping children learn **self**-control. One of the best ways of developing that is to learn to talk out and solve problems and make decisions in the way we have just outlined above.

Concentrating on rules and limits without building a relationship is probably not going to be very effective. If you concentrate on building the relationship with your children, for example, research shows that you will have a much better chance of helping them to say no to sex before marriage. But action may sometimes be called for — perhaps ringing up parents to check that they really will be at home during that party your son has been invited to, or that your daughter really has been asked to babysit. It may also help to limit time spent daily (by you as well as by your children!) sitting passively in front of the television, and to encourage your teenagers to partake in active sporting activities — which has been found to be a good way of releasing sexual energy.

Problem solving in stages

Now, back to the five stages of problem solving as outlined in Table Four. In previous chapters we have become familiar with the first two stages, i.e. with listening and with speaking your own point of view. The third stage is exploring possibilities — coming up with as many suggestions as possible.

In exploring possibilities, it is important to listen to all suggestions — even if your teenager is considering suicide or abortion. Isn't it better to show understanding to someone considering suicide: "It's as bad as that for you — that must be awful" than to say "I'm sorry. I don't want you to talk about that" Being able to talk about their options will actually begin to help your daughter or son to feel better. This does not mean going against your principles. In stage four, when you consider the good and bad results of each suggestion, you will naturally say what your own values are. If you disagree with abortion, you can say so: "I find the very idea of abortion very upsetting, so I obviously can't help you to get one — though I want you to know that I will still love you and respect you."

The fifth and final stage is decision-making. It is best for everyone to be involved in making the

Say what you think and feel.

decision, but at times parents may have to move in and decide what their limits are. When you are dealing with young adults of eighteen plus, however, you cannot make **personal** decisions for them or impose your advice; you may sometimes have to respect their right to make personal decisions you completely disagree with — for example as regards methods of contraception or choice of friends. But you can still stand by your own standards: "I'm sorry. If you want to bring your boyfriend home with you for the Easter break, you will both be very welcome, but you will naturally understand that I cannot accept you sleeping together in my home."

What suggestions can you think of?

Some people have difficulty with the third stage of problem solving — exploring possibilities, so let's look at that now. Here is a real life example written by a parent.

"Our nine year old, Tom, was hearing a lot about sex from his schoolfriend, Alan (who also was only nine!) Alan had told him, among other things, about prostitution, homosexual behaviour, oral sex, and rape (apparently he had got the information from magazines which his father had left lying around — I'm sure the father had no idea what effect they were having!). Tom was fascinated with all this and began to show off his knowledge by making crude remarks to our seven year old daughter — though in fairness he probably didn't realise fully what he was saying. When we discovered what Tom was saying to her, we were shocked and took him aside to talk to him. After some hesitation, he eventually told us where he was getting his information. We told Tom how we felt, and I think it began to register with him how concerned we were. Then, together, we began to write down all possible solutions, even ones we didn't agree with. Here are the suggestions (our own in italics).

Do nothing — just let it blow over.
Tom could change schools
Tom could stop being friendly with Alan
We could talk to Alan
We could punish Tom.
We could talk to Alan's parents.
We could talk to Tom about all his new information on sex.
Tom could tell Alan what we say.

We then went through this list of suggestions, one at a time, and looked at the results of each one. Finally, we agreed that we would talk to Tom about what Alan had told him, and that he would tell Alan he had been talking to us. So it actually became a good opportunity for sex education — and Alan was so shocked that Tom was talking to his parents about things like this that he became distinctly less friendly with Tom."

Sometimes parents will have to step in themselves and decide what the limits are.

Not just to solve a problem

You may not agree with the decision made by Tom and his parents — that was not the important thing. We are all different, and there is no one solution to a problem like this that will suit everybody. But **any** solution is probably a good one when made by caring parents who are doing their best like this.

It is interesting that the first suggestion was to do nothing and let the whole thing blow over. There is a strong temptation to do nothing, particularly to steer clear of areas where you feel inadequate. Some parents, for example, make the mistake of giving their daughter the pill and then retiring into the background — after all, that saves time and talking and bother and it seems to be a liberated thing to do. But where is the sex education there? Where is the challenge, the caring, the encouragement to think and form values?

Or take another common example. Your son is living with his girlfriend, you are not happy with the situation, you feel uncomfortable about it, but times have changed so much since you were young that you don't know what to do. It seems easier to say nothing ("He doesn't listen to me anyway!" or "I'll only seem old-fashioned if I say how I feel." or "It would only make things worse.")

But the purpose of using these skills is not just to solve a problem, nor even to make a stand for your principles. The purpose is to improve your relationship with your son, to listen to him, and to help him think about his situation. So you might begin by encouraging him to talk — perhaps with questions like: "I wonder why you've decided to live together?.. What are the advantages?.. What are the disadvantages?.. Then share how you feel yourself. Perhaps "I feel an awful sense of failure as a parent that you have chosen such different values from mine." You may get no further than that, but talking like this can be a real gift to your son. He may not change his situation, but he will be challenged to think about it and to become clearer about his own values. For that is what happens when we take the time to deal with tensions. Conscience is formed. A greater sense of responsibility develops. Both our children **and** ourselves change and mature and grow in wisdom. And we often get closer to them.

Behaviour

As in previous chapters, it may help to look at the messages we are giving by the way we behave ourselves. After all, how do we teach a crucial sex-education value like the importance of working at relationships if we are not ourselves prepared to make the time to work at our own family relationships? — to listen and talk, to explore together and to plan? Similarly, how do we deal with conflict in our marriage or in our closest relationships? What happens, for example, if a couple has very different sexual needs? There are no rules about frequency of sexual intercourse, of course, but if our needs are different, it can only be helpful to talk about that and consider ways of meeting each other's needs. "Growing in Love" (published Family Caring Trust) has some useful suggestions on how a couple can talk things out when there is conflict.

Sometimes we worry about the effect on children of anger and conflict in the home. A great deal depends, however, on how the arguments are handled. Constant conflict is obviously not a healthy thing, but in the normal family parents will shout at each other or slam the door in a temper from time to time, and it may actually be a good experience for children to see how people can disagree and still manage to work things out together and remain friends. That can be an important part of their sex education.

TABLE FOUR: SOLVING PROBLEMS

It is not necessary to use the five stages of problem solving below for all problems — on some occasions, you may prefer to use just a part of this process. But the usefulness of having a framework like this has to be experienced to be believed. Some parents will be reluctant to write down ideas (stage three), and we respect their right not to — the method can be adapted to make it their own.

---

1. START WITH LISTENING TO CHILD

Most problem solving doesn't work because this crucial stage is left out. Listen. Ask questions. Listen again. Ask more questions. Check out that you have understood. "I'm not sure why you..?" "Can you say a bit more about that..?" "I wonder what makes you say that..?" "Can you help me to understand this point better..?" "How has all that left you feeling..?" "I wonder now if I have grasped what you're saying — is it...?"

---

2. SAY WHAT *YOU* THINK AND FEEL

You have your point of view too. Don't be a doormat. It's important to say what you think and feel. "I've done my best to listen and understand — now I'd like you to give me the same respect. Just hear me out without arguing, and please check out with me that you understand..."

---

3. THINK OF POSSIBLE SOLUTIONS

Both of you — not just one of you — should be thinking of possibilities. It helps to write down the suggestions. Write **any** suggestions, even things that you may not be open to. "Why don't we write down any possibilities we can think of that might meet both our needs — we'll jot down **all** ideas first, and can we agree that there'll be no arguing or criticism of any suggestion at this stage — anything goes." "How can we solve this problem so that you and I can both be reasonably happy..?" "Any other ideas..?"

---

4. LOOK AT GOOD AND BAD RESULTS

It is too easy to be critical. Don't neglect to take time to recognise the strengths and **good** results of each suggestion. It helps to draw a line down the middle of a page, making two separate columns for the good and bad results. "Right, let's look at that first suggestion. What do you see as the advantages there?" "Anything else..?" "I see another advantage in your suggestion..." "Now the disadvantages. What might they be..?" "Any more..?"

---

5. DECISION TIME.

The ideal is a joint decision, but a parent will sometimes have to step in and make a decision (not a life-decision, of course, like the choice of a career). It is important to be specific (who?, what? when? where? for how long? etc.) Consider writing down what is decided — to avoid arguments later. And fix a time for looking at how things are working out in practice. "So which of the possible solutions seems to be the best?" "Why do you say that?" "Is that specific enough?" "Would you like to write down what we've decided?" "When will we look at how things are going?"

COMMENTS FROM PARENTS

I hate them watching these sexy videos. I tell them some of the scenes make me cringe, that I can't bear to watch them myself, that they offend me. But I don't say no. At eighteen and twenty they would just go and watch them somewhere else. And I'd rather have the boys at home and keep the lines open.

One of the best results of this course is the way it has helped me to understand a totally different point of view and realise that I actually have a lot in common with the person who holds that point of view.

I was the boss. Whatever I thought was right was the law. Now I know they have brains of their own.

He knew what was coming. He knew I wanted to talk to him about sex, and he did everything to resist. Last week I felt hopeless, but the breakthrough came on Wednesday evening around the pool table — you can say a lot when you're able to concentrate on something different. Once we got started it was easy. We stopped playing, and I can't believe what a good chat we had and the questions he asked.

The idea of taking pen and paper to deal with problems turned me off. But when we tried it in the group, I could see that writing down the suggestions could be a good idea. Otherwise we wouldn't remember the suggestions and be able to take them one at a time — we'd probably end up talking round in circles.

One of the advantages of being a single parent is that I have got my boys involved in the chores — they cook and iron and wash along with me. I think that should be part of their training.

You can't be a policeman. They're going to start kissing and petting anyway. Your best guarantee is to keep the lines open and get them to talk about it.

I wouldn't have had the confidence to talk to them. Now we're like adults talking about things together.

The course has helped me to face up to things I didn't want to look at. I used to think that sex education was time enough — that problems like these wouldn't come knocking on my door.

GETTING IN TOUCH

Here are a number of situations which some parents fear and would find difficult to cope with. Feel free to add others. Put x for the situations you would find extremely difficult, and a tick for those you feel you might be able to cope with.

Your sixteen year old daughter is keeping company with a man aged twenty seven, whom she says she loves.

Your three year old has been sexually abused by a babysitter.

Your teenage son stays out very late at night.

Your thirteen year old has contraceptives in her schoolbag.

Your unmarried teenager is pregnant.

Your six year old enjoys rubbing his penis in bed.

Your daughter drinks quite a lot at parties.

Your son is homosexual.

Your seventeen year old daughter spends a lot of time in her bedroom with her boyfriend.

CASE STUDY

Your nineteen year old unmarried daughter, a first year student at university, is pregnant, and very upset. She wants to talk things through with you. Write down all the choices you can think of (including choices that you are not open to yourself). Then look at the good and bad results of each choice:

(Parents of younger children may not think this example is relevant to them, but it can actually be easier to deal with a problem in which you are not too closely involved. And remember that the freer you become in talking about a variety of sexual topics with other adults, the freer you will tend to become with your children.)

POSSIBLE CHOICES	GOOD RESULTS	BAD RESULTS
1.		
2.		
3.		
4.		
5.		
6.		
7.		

PLANS FOR NEXT WEEK.

Would you like to mark some of the areas below and plan what changes you might like to make during the next week — the success of the course depends on what you do between sessions. It may help to write down your plans.

1. This week we might look at how we are helping our children with the vitally important task of developing a sense of who they are as sexual persons. For this, there is now overwhelming evidence that children of all ages need to experience limits — even if they only kick against the limits. Natural or self-imposed limits are best, of course. But parents will often need to step in and set limits. What limits do your children have? Would you like to practise the five stages of problem-solving during the coming week? — helping your child to set limits on any of the following (or other) areas: household chores; bedtimes; coming-in times; restrictions on television viewing...

2. On _____ day this week I will have a good chat with one of my children. Bedtime may be suitable for younger children. When might be a suitable time for an older child? See Appendix One for questions to ask, but only choose some that you feel comfortable with).

3. If you have a partner, you may like to choose some questions from Appendix Two.

MY PLANS _____

_____

CHAPTER FIVE: POSITIVE SEX EDUCATION

It was the kind of situation where parents can be thrown completely off balance, for the question was totally unexpected; Ten year old Margaret Wilson had just asked her father:

"What's wrong with rape?"

Margaret's father had the wisdom to turn back the question.

"Where did you come across that word?"

"It says in the paper that a man was put in jail for rape."

"And you don't see anything wrong with that.."

"Was he not allowed to grow rape?"

"Oh... That kind of rape is okay. You see, rape has two different meanings. It's the other kind of rape the man was put in jail for."

"What's the other kind of rape?"

"Well, rape is something very unpleasant, so it's not easy for me to talk to you about it — part of me would like to protect you from this kind of information. You see, I've told you how making love is something very special for your mother and me — where we respect each other and love each other, and want to be close. But rape means **forcing** a woman to have sexual intercourse, so it's like the exact opposite of everything I believe in, and is obviously terribly humiliating and damaging."

What's wrong with rape?

Skills for sex education

In this case there are examples of two of the skills recommended for sex education. First of all, Mr. Wilson turned back Margaret's question. He did not attempt to answer it until he found out where the question was coming from and what was behind it.

Once he had explored a little, of course, he still had to deal with the question — he did not try to fob her off or laugh at her mistake. That brings us to the other important skill he used, namely, talking personally.

Mr Wilson could have answered the question truthfully by saying something like: "Rape is forcing someone to have sexual intercourse." But that might have been a bit bald — giving facts without values. Instead, he chose to speak personally, to say something about rape that he personally felt and believed. There are thousands of different ways to make personal statements, of course; a single parent, for example, might speak personally in quite a different way.

The point is that for Mr Wilson sex education is not just a matter of giving information, nor even preventing future problems. He believes in **positive** sex education, in helping Margaret to form values for living and loving.

He had used two important skills. Other skills we have met include problem solving, setting limits, and (what is probably the skill which most contributes to positive sex education), listening and encouraging our children to say more. Let's consider this example.

Girls don't like me!

Mrs West has recently been making more time to chat to her thirteen year old son, Ron, asking him some of the questions from this book. They had got closer as a result, and Ron now trusts her more. One evening, he said to her:

"I don't think girls like me very much."

It upset Mrs West to hear Ron say that, though it came as no surprise. For a long time she had been aware that Ron had very low self-esteem; it pained her that he could not see himself as he was and that he was so frightened of meeting people. She wanted to reassure him — "Of course girls like you!" But she was convinced of the value of listening and getting her son to say more — and she was pleased that he was now trusting her more.

"You're not sure if girls find you attractive.." she said.

"I didn't say I wasn't sure! I **know** they don't!" he replied, almost angrily. He needed his mother to understand how badly he felt.

"I wonder what makes you say that?.."

He thought for a while.

"I just know.. I'm not good-looking..."

There was a pause. His mother did not try to reassure him — there would be time for that later.

"I'm no good at chatting to girls. I get embarrassed.."

A longer pause this time.

"How long have you felt like this?" — from his mother.

"I don't know. I think.. for years."

Ron was close to tears. Having someone to talk to, someone who listened and understood, was such a relief. He continued on, talking some of the negative feelings out of his system. Eventually he was finished. Mrs West felt it was time now to plant some positive seeds:

"What do you see as your strengths or good points?"

"I suppose.. I'm okay at football."

"Good. What else?.."

"Not much else.." (pause) "Maybe my sense of humour."

"I'm glad you mentioned that, but I mean what are the things that girls might like about you?"

"Aw, mum!.. I don't know!"

"Can I tell you what I like about you?"

"You're biased!"

"Course I am — I know you better than anyone else."

And Mrs West proceeded to tell Ron some of the things she liked about him.

Sex education and self-image

Some healing had taken place for Ron when his mother had given him the opportunity to talk out negative feelings, but it was also important, towards the end of their chat together, to take some time to help him see the positive.

Helping our children to be positive, to think well of themselves and grow in confidence is an essential part of sex education. For it is really difficult for people who do not think well of themselves to love others. And it is very difficult for them to think well of themselves if they have not been loved and encouraged. Indeed, a good deal of sexual experimentation is a vain attempt by young adolescents to find in sex the love and affection and reassurance they missed out on at home. When they tried to get close to their parents as small children, some of them may have felt rejected, so it is easier now to opt for physical sex because they are frightened of being intimate, of getting close to people in any other way. That is why it is often said that sex education begins with the cuddling and warmth and attention a baby receives. Affection frees us to be affectionate.

"I don't think girls like me very much."

Experiencing good attention and listening has another advantage. Children who are listened to and allowed to express negative feelings like anger and jealousy and insecurity are able to get in touch with the underlying positive feelings like friendship, affection and warmth. So a child who has been listened to and loved has a much greater chance of building a caring, honest, lasting relationship with a sexual partner in the future. Happy, confident adolescents are also much less liable to cling to masturbation in an attempt to find their security and comfort.

Parents, then, can probably give their children no greater gift than the sense of security that comes from knowing they are loved. Sweets, toys, music lessons, outings, etc. will never make up for your time and your affection.

We have already seen that merely giving children facts is a very inadequate sex education. Our goal as parents is to help our children grow into mature, self-confident adults, at ease with themselves, with their families and friends, and with members of the opposite sex. We want them to learn to like themselves — including liking being a woman or being a man. For that will give them the confidence to stand up to scoffing, ridicule and the pressure of their peers, such as "You're not a man!" "All the other girls do it." "Everybody else is having it off!"

How we build children's confidence

There is no instant recipe for building this confidence, but the skills highlighted in this book all contribute to it, for they involve taking time to care and understand, to listen and be affectionate, and to encourage children to take increasing responsibility for making their own decisions. In a nutshell, the task of building confidence is to help them to feel **capable**, to feel **responsible**, and to feel **loved**. Perhaps we should look briefly at each of these three things.

1. Able to do some things well

We need to help our children, first of all , to feel capable — able to do at least some things well, to have some basic skills, including communication skills. It helps to be on the look-out for some talent or skill — at music, sport, cooking, schoolwork, anything — and to have a word of encouragement, pointing out the positive. Not that you should aim too high. It may be enough, for a start, to avoid fault-finding, to concentrate on holding your tongue, to cut back on nagging, on scolding, on irritable, impatient, bossy reactions to your children — or on witty remarks that are sarcastic or hurtful. Life is difficult enough for a young person without constant put-downs. All these things damage their confidence in their ability.

2. Responsible for themselves

A second aim is to help children feel responsible for making decisions and living with the consequences. They need to be helped to discuss their choices away from pressures, and

Plan to do something once a week with one child at a time.

to be given increasing responsibility. We looked at some ways of doing this in the last chapter. It is worth noting that helping adolescents to relax, meditate and develop a spiritual dimension in their lives can also help to develop this sense of responsibility — and at the same time this takes a good deal of stress out of their lives.

The sense of security that comes from knowing they are loved.

3. Loved and appreciated

Thirdly, we need to help children to feel loved and cared about, to feel listened to and appreciated. Friendship and warmth enable even a closed, fearful child to open up and trust. Don't worry about finding the right words to encourage. Words are not as important as actions. Make the time for taking young children on your knee and giving them your full attention. Make time for telling them stories. Make time for touching, for a smile and a warm hug — first thing in the morning and last thing at night and just when they come in from school, or when you come home from work. Make time to sit and listen and chat with your children of all ages. That is such an encouraging thing. It says: "You're more important that the TV or the newspaper or my work. You're special to me". Notice your children. Plan to do something once a week with one child at a time — ask them what they would like to do, or what game they would like to play (you may be surprised). Put a surprise chocolate bar into their schoolbags now and again. Thank them. Tease them a little bit. Stay in touch with them. Be available to let them talk about their friends and teachers and the seemingly unimportant little events of their day. Enjoy them — making time may seem like a duty or chore to start off with, but it quickly becomes enjoyable. Go the extra mile with them. Be their best friends. And watch how they blossom and grow in confidence. Wonderful things happen to children when someone is crazy about them.

Remind yourself of the pain

Families are so different that what you have just read may be inspiring for some of you, and it may actually be depressing for others, particularly if your teenagers communicate very little with you. In adolescence, the confidence and self-esteem of young people tends to take a real nosedive and become frighteningly low. They can become so negative and critical. There may be times when you will feel so aggravated and angry with your teenager that you may have no patience left, and the task may seem impossible. You may feel a sense of failure and hopelessness then. This is perfectly normal. Many parents feel it. At times like that, it may help to remind yourself of the insecurity, the fear, and the appalling self-image that lie underneath your teenager's tough front. When they are negative and critical about you it is really because they are feeling critical and hopeless about themselves. Some parents actually find that reminding themselves of that helps them to feel some compassion and be able to go on loving against all the odds.

How you behave

We began this chapter by drawing together the various communication skills that contribute to sex education. Then we moved on to look at one final skill that is particularly crucial — encouragement that builds your child's self image and confidence. As you improve in your use of these skills, of course, you don't just become more effective; you also become a **model** for your children. A model that prepares them for healthy, open relationships in the

There may be times when you will feel so aggravated and angry...

future. For these skills — listening, openness, firmness, gentle questions, problem solving, and encouragement — are all respectful ways of treating people and communicating with them.

It has often been said that when children are listened to they learn to listen. When they are encouraged, they learn to encourage. When you are open with them, they learn to be open in turn. When they are treated with respect, they learn to respect others. That is surely the best way to teach. And the best kind of sex education.

TABLE FIVE: THE THREE PILLARS OF SELF ESTEEM

The three pillars below (based on a Tacade youth programme) all play their part in helping young people feel good about themselves — an essential part of good parenting and of sex education. Your child does not have to be "perfect" before you show approval — it is helpful to notice any little improvement or effort. Which of the three pillars do you think is most important?

1. FEELING CAPABLE

Young people need to feel capable, able to do at least **some** things well, and to have some basic skills, including communication skills.

Examples of skills to encourage: able to sing, wash dishes, do maths, paint, cook, read, cycle, use a screwdriver, swim, play a musical instrument, make friends easily.

2. FEELING LOVED

This is the central pillar. Young people tend to have low self-esteem; they need to feel loved, appreciated, and listened to. They need a lot of encouragement.

Examples of qualities to encourage: kind, good-humoured, hard-working, sincere, friendly, honest, willing, generous, open, helpful, good listener, brave, thoughtful.

3. FEELING RESPONSIBLE

Young people need to feel responsible for making decisions and living with the results of what they decide. It helps to give them increasing responsibility and allow them to discuss their choices away from pressures.

Examples of responsibility to encourage: dresses herself, makes own decision, minds baby, does household chores/homework, comes in on time, prepares own lunch, sensible with drink, cleans bathroom after use..

COMMENTS FROM PARENTS

I have learned such a lot. That sex education is not simply talking about how babies are made. That I need to talk personally to help the children form values. That I needed to talk about sexual intercourse earlier than I had intended. That talking about sex brings us closer to our children — that was so obvious from the feedback.

The course enabled me to talk to my children in a way I had always wanted to but had never got around to.

There was too much crammed into each session. You need time to share things with others, but I often felt rushed. For many women this is the only time they may have someone to talk to.

I've had a great sense of being supported and enriched by everybody — just knowing that others were struggling too and that they also wanted the best for their children.

I'm so glad it combined sex-education with a course on parenting. I couldn't have coped otherwise. I'm still not ready for a lot of the talking about sex, but I'll work at being a better parent for now and I feel hopeful about sex-education in the future — this has given me a sense of direction.

This last session has been very important. I do nag at the children, and I'm sure that will continue, but I know encouragement is right.

I decided that my family was going to be more important then my work. I work at home and tend to get very wrapped up in it, but I now make a few minutes for any of the children who want to talk to me or say hello to me after school. When I have to go somewhere I usually take one of them with me (and — what's hard for me — I switch off the car radio!)

I've gained a lot of confidence in talking about sex both to my husband and my daughters. That's a big change, because I was brought up to believe that sex was dirty.

I think there should be more in the course about preparing young children against sex abuse.

As a single parent, I wondered what I was doing here the first evening, but I quickly realised that couples had the same hang-ups as I had, and I have gained a great deal — I feel I have grown in confidence as a person. I was never at anything like this before — it's been very helpful.

The course has blown the lid off taboo subjects for us. Being in the group has freed me up. I feel I can talk about almost anything now.

I am so thankful for this course because it has removed a great barrier between me and my daughter. I'm delighted with the freedom I have with her, and the closeness that has grown between us.

GETTING IN TOUCH

Based on Table Five, see if you can pick out some strengths or good points in one of your children. Feel free to write other examples that are not in the colums above.

Three skills my child has (see column 1)_____

_____

Three qualities my child has (see column 2)_____

_____

Three ways my child is responsible (see column 3)_____

_____

CASE STUDY

Fourteen year old June is in love, but David, (the object of her love), has just told her friend that he is not interested in June. She is shattered and sees herself as unattractive. Her mother comes home from work to find her in tears. After some hesitation, June tells her what has happened.

Please tick any of the following responses which you think her mother could make to help June recover and believe in herself again. Then underline the one which most appeals to you:

_____ "He's not worth crying over! You'll not be long finding someone else."
_____ "I don't know what you saw in him anyway — his face is covered in spots!"
_____ (hug) "I'm very sorry, June. That's so hard.."
_____ "You're too young to be thinking of boys. You need to concentrate on your exams."
_____ "Of course you're attractive, dear. I never heard anything so silly."

_____ "You're feeling terrible..."
_____ "Is that all you have to worry about!"
_____ "I wonder what makes you say that..."
_____ "I don't blame him!"
_____ (With a twinkle in her eye) "If he knew you as well as I do, he'd be mad about you!"
_____ "Oh, pull yourself together, June — you need to get out and meet people instead of sitting moping around the house!"
_____ Another response?

In small groups of three or four people, have a little chat about what you ticked and why. Respect the points of view of those who differ from you. For example, some parents can do a lot for their children's confidence using humour and a little teasing (without sarcasm); other parents encourage their children to talk out their negative feelings by listening and allowing the child to say more.

PLANS FOR THE FUTURE

Would you like to mark some of the areas below and plan what changes you might like to make for the future. It may help to write down your plans.

1. Can you think of a natural way in which you could build up the confidence and self-image of your most difficult or most discouraged child? Look again at the child's good points that you wrote down, and plan specifically how you will let her/him know that you appreciate these things.

2. What would you like to do about making time for individual chats with your children? Is there an evening in the week, or a time in the evening or at weekends, which might usually suit on an ongoing basis? You might go back a number of times over the questions for children in Appendix One. Parents usually get different answers from the same child at different stages — another reason why sex-education needs to be ongoing!

3. A book should not be a substitute for communication, but it can be a great help. Would you like to choose one from the booklist at the back of this handbook, read it first, and then give it to one of your children? Which book? Which child?

4. We hope that this course has helped to convince you that good parenting is the core of good sex-education. How you behave as a parent — showing affection, encouraging, listening, working out clear limits, making time for talking things through and helping your children to

make responsible decisions — all these would seem to be much more important than merely talking to your child about sex. What one change could you make to build a more encouraging, affectionate atmosphere in your home? (Games, mealtimes, family meetings, outings...)

MY PLANS _____

_____

_____

APPENDIX ONE: QUESTIONS TO ASK YOUR CHILD

Asking good questions would seem to be a much more important part of sex education than giving information. There is room for both, of course — particularly when the information is presented by parents speaking personally.

Bear in mind, however, that **there are years of questions here** — sex education is a lifetime task. For a chat with your child just choose **some** of these questions that you are comfortable with. Decide in advance what questions you want to ask, and write them down or remember them — it is best not to have the book with you when you are asking them, or your child may see the situation as too formal and artificial. It is also important to adapt and change the questions to make them yours — use your own words.

In most sections, the early questions will tend to be suitable for younger children, and the later ones more suitable for teenagers, but this division is not rigid. Many questions are very helpful for all ages. You could decide on some that might be suitable for your children, and mark these with the child's initial.

It often helps to begin a chat about sex by telling your child something from your own personal experience — for example how you learned about sex yourself. Your openness will usually help the child to overcome embarrassment and be more open with you in turn.

Saying no to sexual abuse

(Helping children to have the wisdom and courage to say no is an important area for parents to explore with their children at all ages. But it must be presented positively, distinguishing, for example, between good and bad hugs, and not making young children think that all strangers are evil!)

Some people give you nice touches — good touches — and some people's touches are not so nice — bad touches. Can you give me an example of a good touch? Any others? And a bad touch?.. Any others? Who do you like hugs from? Who do you not like hugs from? I wonder why that is?

Here's a picture of you. Try colouring it in — green for the parts you like to be touched, red for the parts you don't like to be touched... Tell us about that.

(Explore the whole area of "secrets"). I'm going to tell you a secret — I don't want you to tell anyone else, except, of course, people in our family. (Trust your child with a real "secret", like how much you paid for something, or your age, or how much money you earn, or an embarrassing situation you had to deal with).

(Explain the difference between "good" and "bad" secrets). Give me an example of a good secret? And a bad secret? When should you not keep a secret? (In talking about dangers, be relaxed and take care not to show fear — when parents can talk about things without fear, children learn to take "scary" information more in their stride).

If someone asked you to do something you thought was wrong what would you do (run away towards people, yell...?) Who would you tell about it?

What would you say to a stranger who offered you sweets, or money, or a ride in a car?

If someone older than you did something to you that you thought was wrong, whose fault would it be? (It's very important to convince children that any wrong in these circumstances is NOT THEIR FAULT — they are not to blame; for this is why so many children do not tell their parents about sexual abuse).

Handling pressures to have sex

What are some of the things boys/men say to girls/women to put pressure on them to have sex with them? (It's best not to answer this question yourself, but you could add in some of these if necessary — You're the only one for me/ I've never done it with anyone else before/ Everyone else does it — you're a prude/ This will deepen our friendship/ If you really love me you'll say

49

yes/ You've got me all worked up — I can't stop now/ We'll get married) Can you tell me at least four bad effects that might result from putting pressure on someone to have sex?

What are some good ways to resist that pressure? What would **you** do? Let's try a few — I'll say something putting pressure on you, and you decide what you'd say or do...

In what other ways do men force women to have sex with them? (e.g. the majority of teenage pregnancies are drink-related; and it is surprising how many teenagers are not aware that pregnancy can occur without penetration.) What are some practical ways of avoiding situations like this? How do women put pressure on men? (This is increasingly common). What helps in a situation like this?

Your body

What is sex? (If they don't know, there's no need for big explanations — sex can be explained simply as the difference between a man and a woman!) What are the differences? — let's see how many we can get. (Don't just stop at differences in their bodies).

Do you think it matters whether a penis is big or small? Whether breasts are big or small? How do you feel about your body when you're naked? What do you think might help you to feel more positive about it?

(After telling your daughter about a woman's cycle, see appendix three: The Facts) How do you feel now about the fact that you'll have periods — are you glad or embarrassed? What are some reasons to be glad?

Love and maturity

When I was your age, my biggest worry was... What's your biggest worry about growing up? What do you think you could do about that?

(Have a little chat about the "feel, think, act" diagram in chapter two. Ask your child what (s)he thinks it means, and if (s)he can give you an example). Can you give me an example of a choice based on feelings? (fear, pleasure..) Is that immature? Why (not)? Which is harder — to decide to do something, or to do what you decide? Why?

Some people say that, just as we grow in our bodies, we are also made to grow into more loving persons — what do you think that means? Do you think it's true? Can you give me examples of good ways to love in a family? (Bring out that it may be things we don't **feel** like doing). Here's one way I have grown in love.. Tell me a way you have grown in love — a good decision you made when you didn't feel like it.. How do you feel when you make good decisions? And tell me one or two decisions you made that you regret... How did you feel then? What are some bad/good decisions people make in the way they treat the opposite sex? What

happens when someone grows sexually but doesn't grow as a loving person?

How do you feel when you meet boys/girls (the opposite sex)? Do you feel differently with some? What girl/boy do you most admire? What do you like about her/him? How do you know when you're really in love?

What's the difference between loving and being in love? (Tell your own experience of both as well). How do you know when it's really love?

What do you think people mean when they say that a sexual relationship doesn't depend on the amount of time a couple spend in bed together?

Sexual Intercourse

How I met your mother/father. What attracted me to her/him. What it was like to be in love. Why I wanted to get married.

Can you tell me some of the ways we (Mum and Dad) show our love for you? And for each other? Do you like it when we kiss and cuddle each other? What do you like to see us doing? How we enjoy(ed) being close together in bed. How sexual intercourse happens and what a natural way it can be for us to express love.

We're going to talk to your brother/sister about sex. What did you wonder about at that age? (Often reveals what they are wondering about now!)

Some people think that sex is an appetite to be satisfied; others see it more as a way of communicating and caring — what do you think? What difference does that make?

What difference does it make to have sex with someone you're married to and to have sex outside marriage? What do you think people might be communicating in each case?

What do you think people mean when they say that the most important sexual organ is the brain?

Do you know what incest is? (Explain if necessary) Why is it wrong?

Peers

Who's your best friend at present? What do you like about her/him? Do you find it difficult to be different, or to have opinions of your own, at times? Why?

What sex education do you get at school? What do your friends think about that?

What kinds of things do the girls/boys in your class say about sex? (Be prepared for a shock here!)

How have your friends learned about sex?

What do they boast about? How do you feel when you hear them talking like that?

How do boys put pressure on boys to have sexual intercourse with girls? In what ways do girls put similar pressure on girls?

Self Image/Confidence

How I feel about myself, and how that affects me (don't leave out the insecurity and low self-esteem that all of us seem to suffer from at times — it will help your child to understand why you are sometimes moody and sad and why you nag and scold and overreact at times). What helps me to feel better about myself.

Do you like being a girl/boy? What do you think of girls/boys?

Do you think boys like you? Do you think girls like you? What makes you say that? What helps you to have good feelings about yourself?

What do people mean when they say someone has a good personality — what's attractive about that person? (friendly? sincere? sense of humour? good fun? good listener? good talker? cheerful? doesn't laugh at you?) Which of those qualities do you have? Which of them would you like to develop?

What do you like about yourself? Would you like to know what I/ we like about you? (Tell her/him). (Help your children to write down their good qualities and to remind themselves of them regularly).

It's supposed to be harder for people who don't like themselves to get on well with others — do you think that's true? Why do you say that?

Male/Female Roles

(Sex education is about much more than how babies are conceived and born; it's very much about how men and women relate to each other.)

Do you think a mother should stay at home with her children? Or a father? Why? What would you like when you become a parent? Is it possible to have it both ways? What are the difficulties?

Who should be more involved in bringing up children — a father or a mother? What are the advantages of each?

What household chores do you think men should do? Why do you say that? Who will do the chores when you set up home?

What outside work do you think women should do? Gardening?/ mending a fence?/ fixing a TV aerial?.. Why do you say that? How do you feel about "women's liberation"? (If appropriate, you might ask — How do you think Jesus would feel about it?)

Why do you think men find it so hard to say how they feel? What effect does that have?

What are some masculine qualities? And feminine ones? What masculine and feminine qualities do you have? (If appropriate — What masculine and feminine qualities did Jesus have?) What do you think about these qualities — is it fair to call them "masculine" and "feminine"?

Homosexuality

Do you know what it means to be homosexual? Quite a number of people go through a stage of being attracted to people of the same sex — what's the difference between going through a stage like that and being homosexual? Have you ever wondered if you were homosexual?

What do your friends say about people who are homosexual/lesbians? What do they call them? How would you feel if you were gay and people talked like that about you? Do you know anyone who is homosexual? What do you think and feel about them?

What do you see as the difference between being homosexual and having homosexual activity? Why do some churches teach that homosexual activity is wrong? What do you think? Why?

Media

What messages come from the media about sex? (e.g. according to the media, do you have to be married to have sex? When is it okay? What's the tough macho-type man's approach to sex?)

In what ways would you say these messages are different to what we believe? What do **you** think of these messages? Why do you say that?

Why do companies spend so many millions on advertising? In what ways do the media influence people or put pressure on them? — in what they buy? in the clothes they wear? in the music they listen to? in what they do? in how they think? What helps you to stand up to these pressures?

Choices

Do you know what a "wet dream" is?/ what masturbation is? What's the difference? Why do you think people masturbate? How would you compare masturbation to the sex act? Some people say that masturbation is an incomplete use of sex — why do you think they say that? What do you think?

What would you do if you discovered you were pregnant/ if your girlfriend became pregnant?

Why do some women have abortions? What are the arguments for and against abortion?

Do you know the difference between soft porn and hard porn? What effect do you think pornography has on people?

What do you think it is that makes people rape/ become prostitutes?.. Anything else?..

Do you know how sexual diseases are passed on? What would prevent that? Anything else? What do you think is the best way to prevent it?

Can you think of anything you could possibly do that I could not forgive you for? (If appropriate, you could also ask if there is anything they think God would not forgive them for)

Dating

Which do you think is best — going around in a mixed group, or one to one dating? Why do you say that? What are the advantages of young people going around in a mixed group?

At what age do you think boys and girls should start dating singly? Why do you say that?

What do girls expect of boys on a date? What do boys expect of girls? Tell me as many reasons as you can think of why young people date? How would you like to be treated on a date? How would you let your "date" know what you expect?

What advice would you give to someone before their first date?

What's the difference between light and heavy petting? What do you think about them? (Some parents have found it helpful to push a heavy book very slowly over the edge of a table until it crashes to the floor — to illustrate how heavy petting can suddenly get out of control). What would you do if you were raped on a date? Is date-rape as serious as rape by a stranger? Why do you say that?

Marriage

What boy/girl do you like best/ Would you like to marry him/her? What kind of husband/wife would you like?

What makes a good husband? What makes a good wife? What kind of wife/ husband do you think you will be? How would you like your marriage to be different from ours? Who should make the decisions in a marriage? Which of us (father/mother) makes most decisions? Why do you say that?

What do you not like Mum/Dad and me to do? How do you feel when we have rows? What makes you feel insecure or frightened in our family?

If you were married and had £200 per week coming in, how do you think you would spend it (how much on entertainment, clothes, house, food, etc). What would you do if your husband/wife disagreed with you on that?

Do you think sex will be an important part of your marriage? Can you explain what you mean? What sex means for me/ us.

(Share some of the disappointments and joys of being married). What are the main difficulties facing married people today? What are the pluses? What does it mean that a marriage has to be worked at?

Do you think it's important to be a virgin before marriage? Why do you say that? What are the advantages and disadvantages of living together before marriage?

Sexual Slang

I'd like to have a little chat about the "rude" words you hear. What "rude" words have you heard people using?.. (Explain them, or promise to find out). Why do you think people say that these words are "rude" or vulgar? How do these words get across the idea that men are superior and women are inferior? that men are active and women are mere passive sex objects

that things are "done" to? What's the difference between treating a woman as a "sex object" and treating her as a person?

How I learned about slang words myself. How I feel about them. Do you know the proper names of boys'/ girls' private/ sexual parts? (It may help to use the diagram in Appendix Three for explaining).

What do you think about people who use four-letter words a lot? Do you see it as a stage people go through or something that's quite normal for mature people?

Family Planning

My pregnancy with you — what I remember of it. My memories of your babyhood and childhood. How many children I wanted.

How many children would you like to have? Why?

My experience of family planning. How to achieve or avoid pregnancy. (Parents who use natural methods of family planning have found it helpful to show their charts to their teenage children — this can help to make them more aware of fertility, even aware of how pregnancy can occur without penetration).

How tampons are used.

Methods of family planning — their advantages and disadvantages (ask about this as far as possible — don't just tell. Use the information in Appendix Four if it helps).

APPENDIX TWO: FOR COUPLES TO CHAT ABOUT

*You will gain great freedom in chatting about sex with your child when you become freer in chatting about sex to other adults, but especially to your own partner, if you have one. Many people believe that one of the best possible forms of sex education is just exposing a child to an ordinary couple who love each other and are increasingly free with **each other** in talking personally about sex. So here are some questions a couple might chat about. The suggestion is that you allow your partner to talk for a few minutes about one or more of these questions, without interruption, and then check out that you have grasped what (s)he has said. Then you take your turn speaking without interruption.*

After Session One
* My feelings after reading chapter one.
* How I learned about where babies come from/ sexual intercourse/ masturbation/ homosexuality.
* How I feel about talking to you about sex.
* How I feel about talking to the children about sex.
* What I like about you and about being married to you.

After Session Two
* My feelings after reading chapter two.
* How I really feel about myself as a person (including what I like and dislike about myself, and how I feel about myself as a sexual partner).
* How I would rate myself on a scale of 1-10 as a listener. Why.
* Where, when and how I most like you to touch me.

After Session Three
* My feelings after reading chapter three.
* How I feel about talking **personally** to the children about sex.
* How I feel about having sexual intercourse with you at unusual times and places
* What effect sex on television has on me. And what effect I think my television viewing habits have on the children.
* How I feel about the shape of my body — and how I feel when I am nude with you.

After Session Four
* My feelings after reading chapter four.
* The sexual behaviour I would most fear in one of the children.
* How I feel before, during and after we make love. What I would like to be different.
* Where, what time of day and how often I would like us to make love. (If you feel very differently about this, why not try the five stages for problem solving — from chapter four.)

APPENDIX THREE: THE FACTS

by Sheila Campbell, wife, mother and marriage counsellor

Egg and Seed

When a girl is born, she has enough eggs to last her for the whole of her fertile life. They are the size of a pin head and the two places where they are stored are called her **ovaries**.

About the age of eleven, when a girl's first period arrives (**puberty**) the ovaries begin to release the eggs and her fertile life begins. It ends around the age of fifty with her change of life or menopause. During those years she is capable of making a baby if a man's seed (or **sperm**) should meet (or **fertilise**) one of her eggs.

Monthly Cycle

Each month, about two weeks before her period, an egg leaves one of the two ovaries and travels along a tube towards her womb. The womb gets ready by preparing its lining to receive a baby. After a few days, the womb realises that it is not going to have a baby, so it sheds its lining, its preparation and the unfertilised egg. It takes a few days for these to drip away, in the form of blood, through the neck of the womb, down the front passage (or vagina). Then, two weeks later, the process starts again — another egg leaves the other ovary, the womb makes its preparations again, and the period follows if conception doesn't occur. This is called the "Monthly Cycle".

In theory, there are only 4 or 5 days in the month when the egg can be fertilised. For the rest of the month a couple can make love but they cannot make a baby. Science is now helping couples to learn to recognise certain signals coming from the woman's body so that they can make or put off making a baby.

Puberty in Boys

A boy too is born with seed-making (or **reproductive**) parts. These seed-making parts are in a little bag under his **penis** and are called his **testicles**. The seeds/sperm are produced in thousands although only one is needed to fertilise an egg. They pass out through his penis — usually every two weeks, in a "wet dream" during his sleep. Because they are outside his body, the increase in the size and activity of the sexual parts is more noticeable in the growing boy. The changes in a boy are also much more

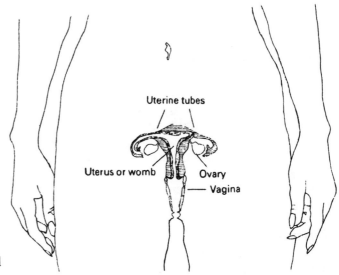

Uterine tubes

Uterus or womb

Ovary

Vagina

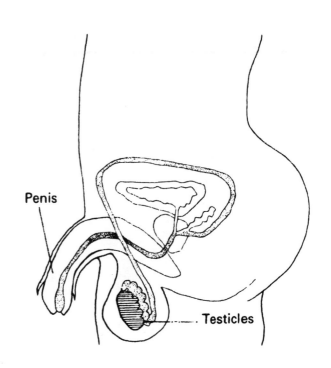

Penis

Testicles

dramatic and bewildering and his sexual feelings are more to the surface than the girl's, so he needs a lot of adult help to understand, to accept and to control them and to realise that such control is both manly and strong.

The couple

Sexual feelings help to attract men and women to each other in different kinds of friendships but they find their fullest expression in the act of loving sexual intercourse in marriage. Here a couple, who have promised to develop their love for each other for life can find the closeness, the support and the healing that helps them to keep on growing in love.

That does not happen automatically, of course. The security of a promise for life helps, but a couple must also go on creating the best conditions for their love to grow, sharing ideas and feelings, communicating in words and without words. The physical expression of their love is a vital part of that sharing and can reach its peak when a woman receives the man's seed from his penis through her vagina in a joining that is loving and intimate.

Pregnancy

Pregnancy begins when an egg and sperm meet through a couple's lovemaking. The preparations which the womb makes each month are then needed to nourish the new life. The baby takes shape quickly, cradled in a bag of water within the womb, closely linked to the mother and receiving food and oxygen through the **umbilical cord**. It is thought that the growing baby is even affected by the mother's changing moods and feelings.

Around the sixteenth week of pregnancy the mother can feel her baby move; a few months later, the movement becomes stronger and the father too can feel his developing child. A baby born after twenty eight weeks (or even up to five weeks earlier) can live; if it comes away before that, the mother is said to have a **miscarriage**. Of course, the longer it stays in the womb, up to the thirty sixth week, the healthier it is likely to be.

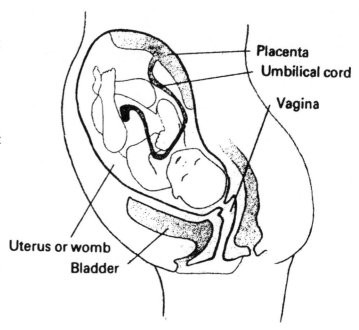

A Baby is Born

Labour begins around the fortieth week. The name is a good one, for although medicine has done away with most of the pain, it takes a lot of hard work to bring a baby to birth. During the first stage, the muscles of the womb tighten and loosen in order to open the neck and allow the baby's head to pass through. These contractions come faster as the second stage approaches — the baby slowly makes its way head-first through the vagina, pushed along by each strong contraction until it finally slips through. A baby is born. Birth is quite a shock. (S)he feels helpless, cold and hungry, totally dependent on parents for food, warmth and closeness. Sex education begins for the child with the experience of being loved and cared for.

APPENDIX FOUR:
METHODS OF FAMILY PLANNING

Contraception is quite freely available as an option for young people today, so it is important to discuss it. Otherwise young people will go elsewhere for their information — and for their values. Below is a brief description of how the various methods work.

Diaphragm/Cap: These work by creating barriers in the vagina (diaphragm) or at the cervix (cap) in order to stop sperm from getting to the ovum (or egg). With careful use, this method is 85-97% effective when used with **spermicides** (creams, jellies, etc., that are put into the vagina and act by killing the sperm cells).

Condom or sheath: This is a male barrier method with the same purpose; the condom is placed over the penis to prevent the sperm from reaching the ovum. Sperm can sometimes escape through a faulty sheath or at the opening. 85-98% effective when used carefully.

The Pill (or oral contraceptive): When taken regularly, the combined pill acts by stopping ovulation (the release of the egg), disturbing the lining of the womb, and providing a barrier of thick mucus at the cervix. If a breakthrough ovulation should take place, this pill also prevents a fertilised egg from being implanted. There is some concern about side-effects — it is not recommended for everyone, especially women over 45, smokers over 35, and people with certain medical conditions. More than 99% effective when taken properly.

Mini-pill: Has the same effect as above but only stops ovulation in a small percentage of cycles. Thus its main effect is to create a barrier and to prevent a fertilised ovum from being implanted. 98% effective when taken properly.

IUD/ IUCD/ Coil : A loop, bow, ring or spiral inserted by a doctor and left in the womb. It may or may not prevent conception, and if conception takes place, it prevents the fertilised egg from settling in the womb. 96-99% effective.

Male sterilisation (vasectomy): This has the effect of preventing the man from emitting sperm that can fertilise the female egg. The operation is irreversible under normal circumstances, so the effect is permanent. 99.9% effective.

Female sterilisation (tubal ligation): An operation to tie a woman's tubes so that an egg cannot pass to meet the sperm. It is normally irreversible. It can have some physical and psychological side-effects. 99.7% effective.

NATURAL METHODS

Withdrawl: Involves interrupting sexual intercourse by spilling the seed. It is unreliable and generally unsatisfactory.

Calendar or Rhythm method: This depends on a couple not making love during the fertile days of the cycle — based on the assumption that the woman's cycle is regular and will continue to be regular. It is based only on an assumption and not on scientific evidence.

Ovulation (Billings) method: By recording on a chart the mucus changes at her vagina, a woman can pinpoint the fertile and infertile times in her cycle and thus know when to abstain from sexual intercourse. This is a reliable scientific method when used properly, but it needs to be learned from someone who is experienced and trained to help — not from a book.

Temperature method: By taking her temperature each morning, a woman can also pinpoint the fertile and infertile times in her cycle. This is often combined with the ovulation method as a double-check method. It is then known as the sympto-thermal method. 85-93% effective when used carefully. These last two methods are the only ones encouraged by the Roman Catholic Church.

MORE BOOKS

*Rather than swamp you with too many books, we include here only a small selection of the many books available on sex education. It can be very helpful to read **some** books, for they are useful in helping us to develop clearer values about sex. Those below have been grouped into two sections — books for parents/ couples, and books which parents might give to their children as one way of encouraging the children also to form values. Some of these books are suitable both for parents and for their children.*

BOOKS FOR PARENTS

General

"Parents Listen" by Lucienne Pickering. Emphasis on communication between parents and their children while placing sex in the context of love. Written by a youth counsellor and mother, this book contains a lot of wisdom and commonsense. Recommended. Publ. Geoffrey Chapman, London.

Books in the Christian tradition

"Intended for pleasure: sex technique and sexual fulfilment in Christian marriage" Recommended for couples. Publ. Scripture Union.

"I married you" by Walter Trobisch. Publ. Inter-Varsity Press, Leicester.

"How to help your child say no to sexual pressure" by Josh McDowell. A well-argued book. Recommended especially because it puts sex education into the context of parenting. Could be discouraging for some parents because it is a little idealistic in parts, but there are also many practical suggestions. Publ. Word Publishing, Milton Keynes.

Books in the Roman Catholic tradition

"Parents talk love: the Catholic Family Handbook about Sexuality" by Susan Sullivan and Matthew Kawiak. A well-researched, helpful book for parents with a good deal of information and how to present it at the various stages of a child's development. Publ. Paulist Press, New York.

"Becoming a man" by William Bausch / "Becoming a woman" by Valerie Dillon. Both published Twenty Third Publications, Connecticut, and Columba Press, Dublin. Two companion books that are thoughtful and thought-provoking for both parents and their children. Although written by Roman Catholics, people from other Christian traditions will find much to think about in these pages. A little directive and "teachy" in parts, but good explanations of Christian values in relation to sex.

Special Areas

"Sex and the Single Parent" by Jane Adams. Publ. Coward, McCann & Geoghegan, N. York.

A Family Matter: "A Parent's Guide to Homosexuality" by Charles Silverstein. Publ. McGraw-Hill, New York.

"Taught Not Caught" Strategies for Sex Education. A book for people interested in teaching sex education in schools, youth clubs, etc. Many practical ideas, some of which we have found useful in developing this programme. Publ. Learning Development Aids. Wisbech, Cambs.

There is a section on sex education and the disabled in "What to say after you clear your throat; A Parent's Guide to Sex Education" by Jean S. Gochros. Publ. Press Pacifica, Hawaii.

BOOKS TO GIVE YOUR CHILDREN

Giving your children a book should not be a substitute for communicating, but it can be a good help; when you give your daughter or son one of the books below, that in itself is a statement that sex is good, something you want them to know about, something that is not taboo, and that you are open to talking about. It is recommended that you yourself read a book before giving it to your children or sharing it with them — you will then have a better chance of communicating about it.

General

We suggest that parents browse through the considerable selection of books, many of them in colour and lavishly illustrated, in larger bookshops. It should not be difficult to find something they are happy with to suit different ages. Here are just a few:

"Where do babies come from?" by Jill Kenner. A best-selling book for children about eight or nine years old.

"Girls talk" and its companion, "Boys talk" by Lucienne Pickering. Written for young people aged 10-12 or earlier, these two very readable books complement "Parents listen" above, and have a sensitive, caring, responsible approach. Publ. Geoffrey Chapman, London.

"Are you there, God? It's me, Margaret" by Judy Blume. a very popular book with early teens which parents would do well to read first, then give to their children — a great way to get talking about sexual values. Publ. Pan.

"Forever" by Judy Blume. This is the story of two seventeen year olds who fall in love and have sexual intercourse. It raises some good issues for discussion. Your teenager is probably going to read this book anyway, so, again, it is suggested that you read it first, give it to your son or daughter, and use it as a springboard for chatting about sexual values. Publ. Pan.

Books/Videos in the Christian tradition

"What is love" by Patrick Berry. A book parents can use along with younger children to introduce them to the basic facts of sex and set them in a religious context. Publ. Mayhew-McCrimmon.

"Sex and that: What's it all about" by Michael Lawson and Dr. David Skipp. A simply written, engaging book, includes comic strips, for teens and pre-teens. Publ. Lion.

"Lessons in Love" by Steve Chalke. A video aimed at committed Christians. Seven talks. Useful with 14-16 year olds. The video itself is not as important as the discussion after each section on the standards and values it promotes — even the reaction to those. Publ. Care, 53 Romney St., London SW1P.

Books/Videos in the Roman Catholic tradition

"Becoming a man"/ "Becoming a woman" See details above. Written both for parents and for their adolescent children. A good 15th/16th/17th birthday present.

"Sex education for girls" by Angela Macnamara. A helpful video in six sections that can be watched along with your child — preferably well before adolescence. Parents should make time to watch it first. Then they can watch just one section at a time with their daughter, making time for a chat after each viewing. (A companion video is planned for boys). Publ. Veritas, Dublin.

GROUNDRULES

Those taking part in this programme tend to feel safer when the following groundrules are agreed right from the start.

1. **Take it seriously** Those who work hard at the skills between sessions tend to draw closer to their children.

2. **No pressure** Some people are naturally shy and reluctant to speak, even in a small group. Obviously, the more open you can be, the better, but no one at any stage has to talk in the group.

3. **Encourage others to speak** This groundrule is for the person who tends to talk too much. Please don't speak a second time about any topic until everyone has at least had an opportunity to speak once. Hogging the conversation can spoil the course for others. Please draw others out and encourage them to talk first.

4. **Respect people's confidences** It is important to respect people's trust and not to talk to anyone else about what you hear in the group.

5. **Take it slowly** Don't let discouragement beat you if you make mistakes or seem to be slow about getting results. Learning new skills takes time and patience. You will probably meet strong resistance from your teenagers initially, but keep leading into topics as gradually and as naturally as possible — it is probably best not to tell them that you are doing a course or their guard may go up unnecessarily.

6. **No preaching** There is no one way to deal with children. Please respect people's right to their own approach and their own opinion. What works for you may not work for them. Feel free to say what works for you but please don't advise others or preach.

SUPPORT FOR THE FAMILY

Every year, a great deal of effort and a great many millions of pounds are spent on attempts to cope with family breakdown. Yet the breakdown continues to increase, and society faces hugh problems as a result of it — ever-growing crime rates and drug addiction, broken marriages, broken homes, bitterness . . .

Very little money is spent on preventing the problems arising in the first place, though that might be a very wise investment.

Recently, however, there has been a growing awareness of this need, and initiatives are beginning to appear. Parents who felt confused, even hopeless, are today being given skills and self-confidence. Family Caring is helping to make that happen. It is a non-profit organisation for the preventive care of the family, registered as a Charity in the UK and operating across Britain and Ireland. Family Caring is responsible for the design, testing and production of practical programmes for families from all social backgrounds — from the most prosperous families to the least privileged. As well as that, it co-operates with schools, churches, social services and voluntary organisations, providing training and ongoing support in implementing the programmes. In just a few years it has already reached ten of thousands of parents and couples and given them some hope.

PARENTING

The Veritas Basic Parenting Programme

This is a programme of eight weekly sessions that enables parents (of children aged 2-20) to improve their skills and create a framework of discipline and respect in their families.

It is the Trust's most popular programme and has been adopted by hundreds of community — based groups and by more than a thousand schools or parent-teacher groups (as an outreach to parents of children attending their schools).

The boxed kit includes 5 cassette tapes, 8 posters, a leader's guide and one parent's handbook.

The Teen Parenting Programme

This course of six weekly sessions reinforces the same skills as the basic parenting programme while dealing with the more difficult situations met in the teen years. It is recommended, but not essential, that parents of teenagers experience the basic programme first, for this is an ideal follow-up to the basic one.

The kit includes 4 cassette tapes, 6 posters, a leader's guide and 1 parent's handbook.

MARRIAGE SUPPORT

The "Married Listening" Programme

Many initiatives offering marriage support meet a major stumbling block when they experience the difficulty of attracting husbands. This programme, however, offers four weekly sessions for groups of married women *without* their husbands, and the results are surprisingly positive — about 50% of husbands to date have been so pleased with the *effects* that have rubbed off on them that they have then become open to experiencing a course for couples. The programme can also be run for groups of husbands or for groups of couples.

Again, this course reinforces similar skills to those of the parenting programmes, so it can be a good follow-up for parents who have attended a parenting course, many of whom are women anxious to involve their husbands in any case.

The boxed kit includes 2 cassette tapes, a leader's guide, and one participant's handbook.

SEX EDUCATION

The 'Parenting and Sex' Programme

Possibly the best follow-up to a parenting course, and one that parents often express a need for. This five session course enables parents to learn skills for talking and listening to their children (of all ages) about sex. It also looks at ways of dealing with difficult areas like dating, late-night discos, television–viewing, peer pressure...

The kit includes a leader's guide and a parent's handbook.

THESE MATERIALS ARE AVAILABLE ONLY FROM FAMILY CARING TRUST